На Пречестный Клейнотъ Герковный Кнзей
ГОЛИЦИНОВЪ

Камо бежиши воине избранный,          Не ты но Образъ Кнза преславнаго,
Многады слане чтто венчанны,          Вовсаки страна, Зде начортанаго,
Трудовъ сицевый, и воинской крани,     Онинъ будетъ славою слати,
Вечно ти славы дотеше претани.         Четь Голицанов везде прославати

Russian Biography Series, 14

# RUSSIA AND THE WEST, THE LIFE OF A SEVENTEENTH-CENTURY WESTERNIZER, PRINCE VASILY VASIL'EVICH GOLITSYN (1643-1714)

by

## LINDSEY A.J. HUGHES

Oriental Research Partners
Newtonville, Mass
1984

© ORP, 1984

All rights of reproduction in any
form whatsoever are reserved by
the publisher.


ISBN: 0-89250-147-2
Library of Congress No.: 84-060061


This is Number 14 in our Russian
Biography Series. For a catalogue,
write to Dr. P. Clendenning
Editor, ORP, Box 158, Newtonville
Mass. 02160.

To Stuart Sinclair

# CONTENTS

## NOTE ON TRANSLITERATION

A modified Library of Congress system has been adopted, omitting diacritical marks. In the English text in proper names Ya- and Yu- replace initial Ia- and Iu- (e.g. Yaroslavl', Yury) and -ii endings are replaced by -y (e.g. Vasily, Shaklovity).

All translations are my own unless otherwise indicated.

L.A.J.H

## NOTE ON MEASUREMENTS/MONEY

### Linear measures

1 chet'(chetvert') = 4.1 acres
1 verst = .663 miles

### Money

1 ruble = 100 Kopeks
1 altyn' = 3 Kopeks
1 den'ga = ½ Kopek

# INTRODUCTION

Prince Vasily Vasil'evich Golitsyn[1], was born in the 1640s, probably in or near Moscow. His active career was comparatively brief; having held a number of conventional appointments at court in his youth, in 1676 he was made a boyar by the new tsar Fedor and sent on a military mission to the Ukraine, where he served on and off until 1681. With the establishment of the regency of Tsarevna Sophia Alekseevna, sister of the underaged tsars Ivan V and Peter I, in May 1682, he assumed control of Russia's foreign affairs and became the regent's chief minister and possibly her lover. He fell from power in September 1689 when his patroness was ousted by the 17 year-old Peter I and spent the rest of his life in exile. He died and was buried near the town of Pinega on April 21 (1714)

The uncertainty surrounding the date and place of birth of so eminent a statesman is characteristic of the era and country into which he was born, as is his failure to leave for posterity the sort of personal record which the biographer of a contemporary Western European politician might expect to have at his disposal.[2] In the 1640s Russia had still not fully recovered from the upheaval of the Time of Troubles and showed few signs of emerging from her "medieval" backwardness. The customary difficulties of administering Muscovy's vast territories with poorly educated personnel and inadequate communications were compounded by the burdens of foreign wars and frequent disturbances amongst the peasantry, townspeople and tribute-paying natives which drained the treasury and strained the already overloaded bureaucracy and army. In 1649 a new code of laws, the Ulozhenie, reiterated the principles of autocracy, consolidated the institution of serfdom and imposed harsh penalties for a wide range of offences. In the same year the burning of six carriages-full of "diabolical" musical instruments gives just one indication of the firm control still wielded by the Orthodox Church in cultural and intellectual matters.[3] In the 1640s Russia maintained no permanent embassies in foreign states, had no establishment of higher education and practically no secular learning or art. It is not surprising, then, that in the West Russia, if considered at all, was regarded as backward and barbaric, her government despotic and her people more akin to the infidels of the East than to Christians. The few intrepid travellers who visited the country generally confirmed these preconceptions. For example, Adam Olearius, who first visited Russia in the 1630s, wrote: "If a man consider the natures and manner of life of the

1

Muscovites, he will be forc'd to avow, there cannot any thing be more barbarous than that people... The ill education they have when young, never learning any thing beyond reading and writing, and certain vulgar prayers, makes them blindly follow that which in Beasts is called Instinct; so that Nature being in them depraved and corrupted, their whole life must needs be a constant course of viciousness."[4]

It is likely that few, if any, foreigners were aware that during Golitsyn's youth a number of events were to signal the imminent opening of that "window on the West" which Peter the Great was later credited with establishing. In the 1650s-60s, for example, Patriarch Nikon's attempts to reform corrupt religious rituals and texts created a schism amongst the faithful which irrevocably weakened the Church, destroying its last claims to political influence and loosening its domination of learning. In the same period the annexation of the Ukraine to Muscovy and war with Poland (1654-67) brought Russia into contact with Orthodox neighbors in both the Ukraine and Belorussia, whose closer proximity to the West had produced higher levels of education and cultural sophistication. In the meantime links with Europe multiplied as the Muscovite government's need of trained personnel brought in a steady stream of soldiers, engineers, merchants, weapon-makers and other craftsmen. In 1652 a separate district of Moscow -- the Nemetskaia Sloboda -- was allocated to the tsar's foreign employees.

These changing circumstances were accompanied by a series of innovations which, although still on a small scale, heralded the more comprehensive changes of Peter's reign. In 1649, for example, a translation of a German work on the art of warfare appeared amongst the overwhelmingly religious output of Moscow's only printing press, to be followed by other secular "firsts" such as the printing of the Ulozhenie in 1649 and the first history of Russia, Innokenty Gizel's Synopsis, in 1674. In 1667, the year that Patriarch Nikon was deposed and the city of Kiev acquired temporarily from Poland, Dutchmen built Russia's first ship, the Eagle, and a foreign merchant set up a postal service to the West. 1672, the year of Peter's birth, saw both the first theatrical performances at court and the dispatch of Russia's largest ever diplomatic delegation to European states to seek allies for Poland's war with Turkey. Innovations at court and amongst the higher nobility included the small-scale introduction of portraiture from life, canvasses and murals on secular themes and Western fashions in architecture, furnishings and clothing. In 1682 Golitsyn himself headed the commission that proposed the abolition of the Code of Prece dence, the system of allocating government appointments according to the candidate's pedigree and family service record, whilst a little later, during Sophia's regency, the first seat of higher education -- the Slavonic-Greek-Latin Academy -- began to function in Moscow.

In the light of all this it is not hard to see why historians have generally characterised the latter half of the seventeenth century as an "age of transition", a "period of preparation for Peter's reforms" and so on. D.S. Likhachev's notion of a belated "Renaissance" has also gained currency.[5] Within this scheme Golitsyn figures prominently amongst a small group of "new men" who stood out amongst their more traditionally-minded contemporaries for their adoption of Western ways, their erudition and culture, their Western-oriented politics or a combination of all three. At the height of his career he was described by a foreign visitor as "without doubt one of the most intelligent, the most refined and most magnificent men that this country, which he intended to set on a par with others, has ever seen."[6] The nineteenth-century historian S.M. Solov'ev considered him "more impressive and capable than any of the boyars of his age",[7] and V.O. Kliuchevsky described him as "a fervent admirer of the West... for which he renounced many of the cherished traditions of Russian antiquity."[8] More recently he has been seen as "one of the chief architects of the reform movement on the eve of much wider, deeper and more important reforms of the late 17th-early 18th century,"[9] and "an important link between the Westernising world of Alexis and that of Peter."[10] Examples could be multiplied, but those quoted should serve to establish Golitsyn's credentials as a worthy subject for biography, both as "man of his era" and as a personality in his own right. A number of short and often inaccurate biographical sketches were published before the Revolution,[11] but in more recent times Golitsyn has rarely made more than a token appearance in general histories and at the beginning of biographies of Peter I. The present study aims to present a more detailed examination of Golitsyn's career than has yet been undertaken, and also to reach some conclusions about the man himself, whose elusive image can be extracted only with difficulty from the meager records that survive. To quote again from De la Neuville, he wished to "colonise the deserts, enrich beggars, transform savages into men, cowards into heroes and herdsmen's huts into stone palaces."[12] The fact that Golitsyn failed to realise most of his more grandiose aspirations makes him no less interesting a subject for the historian's attention.

# CHAPTER ONE

## EARLY YEARS

The Golitsyn family, one of the largest and best known of Russian princely clans, traces its ancestry to Gedymin, Grand Prince of Lithuania, who reigned from 1316-41, and through him to Vladimir, Grand Prince of Kiev, who brought Christianity to Russia in 988.[1] An official heraldry compiled in the reign of Paul I stated: "Many of the princes Golitsyn, in both ancient and modern times, won glory for their clan by heroic deeds and labors undertaken for the sake of the Fatherland, in both military and civil service; and they were rewarded with orders and other marks of distinction and with the monarch's favor."[2] The family name is probably derived from the word <u>golitsa</u>, a leather gauntlet, and was first borne by Mikhail Ivanovich Golitsa, who served under both Tsars Vasily III and Ivan IV and died in 1554.[3] Another notable ancestor was our subject's namesake, Prince Vasily Vasil'evich, dubbed "pillar of the Fatherland", who was a candidate for the throne during the Time of Troubles and died in captivity in Poland in 1619.[4] The family tree branched out with Prince Andrei Andreevich (died 1638) whose four sons founded the divisions of the clan from which all subsequent Golitsyns are descended. The progenitor of the senior branch and our subject's father, Prince Vasily Andreevich (died 1652) has a less distinguished service record than his brothers. He held conventional court appointments and although some historians refer to him as a boyar, contemporary sources do not record this fact. As N. Ustrialov noted, even the Golitsyn genealogy compiled by order of Tsarevna Sophia Alekseevna in honor of her favorite omitted any reference to his father's boyardom.[5] Apart from the bare bones of his career, we know nothing of the character or talents of Prince Vasily's father or of his influence upon his more distinguished son. He died when Vasily was still a boy, leaving his wife, the noblewoman Tat'iana Ivanovna Streshneva to see to her son's upbringing, no doubt with the aid of his uncles, especially Aleksei, who was later serving as military governor of Kiev when his nephew embarked upon his first important posting.

The year of Vasily Vasil'evich's birth has not been established with certainty. The author of a short article published in 1886 claimed to have transcribed the admittedly "badly worn" inscription on Golitsyn's tombstone recording that the prince died in 1714 in the 69th year from his birth,[6] but subsequent writers have not accepted this information. The date 1643 is accept-

# G O L I T S Y N   F A M I L Y   T R E E

ANDREI ANDREEVICH
(? - 1638)
m. EVFIM'IA YUR'EVNA PEL'EMEVAIA-SABUROVA

VASILY
(?-1652)
m. TAT'IANA
IVANOVNA STRESHNEVA

IVAN
(?-1690)

ALEKSEI
(1632-94)

MIKHAIL
(1639-87)

GEORGY

IVAN

VASILY
(1643-1714)

m.(2) EVDOK'IA
IVANOVNA STRESHNEVA

IRINA

PRASKOV'IA

IRINA
(1663-1701)

ALEKSEI
(1665-1740)

EVDOK'IA
(1677-?)

PETR
(d. before
1687)

IVAN
(d. before
1687)

MIKHAIL
(c.1689-?)

5

ed by the official family historian N.N. Golitsyn,[7] and appears in standard Soviet reference works.[8] The earlier date of 1633 given in a number of works would make Golitsyn an unusually late developer in view of the known facts of his career,[9] whilst there seems to be no evidence for the 1639 date supplied in another work.[10] Information about Prince Vasily's siblings is also scanty. N.N. Golitsyn records that he had two brothers, one of whom probably died in infancy, and two sisters, of whom only Irina appears in our sources in letters to her brother in the year 1677.[11] The surviving brother, Ivan, may have been military governor of Kazan in 1686.[12]

In the absence of records about Golitsyn's early life -- a common problem in the biographies of even the most eminent seventeenth-century Russians -- we can only assume that his childhood followed the customary pattern for one of his background, brought up in or near Moscow and groomed for future government service. In the absence of schools, instruction received at home would have been in basic reading and writing skills derived from alphabet primers and later from study of the catechism, psalter and other materials of mainly religious content. The mature Golitsyn's mastery of foreign languages, especially Latin, and his interest in politics and history were almost certainly acquired later in life, although it is not beyond the bounds of possibility that he may have come into contact with one or more of the "Polish" tutors whose employment he was later to advocate to the Russian nobility.[13] The most likely scene of such contact would have been at court. In 1664, for example, the Byelorussian churchman and poet Simeon Polotsky (1629-80) settled in Moscow, becoming tutor to Tsarevich Aleksei in 1667 and, after the latter's death, to Fedor and Sophia, to whom he taught, amongst other things, Polish and verse composition.

Golitsyn first entered court service in about 1658 when, according to some sources, he was employed as table attendant (stol'nik) and cupbearer (chashnik).[14] For a servitor of Golitsyn's tender years these titles can be taken fairly literally, involving the holder in attendance on the tsar and participation in ceremonials and day-to-day rituals. Golitsyn's aristocratic status assured him of, indeed obliged him to accept such posts, traditionally held by members of his class, and later to undertake military or bureaucratic responsibilities in Moscow or the provinces. Nor was the early age of Golitsyn's summons exceptional; his own son Aleksei was to enter the tsar's retinue at the age of 12. Adolescent aristocrats from Moscow's leading families were customarily "groomed" at court, and lack of a summons may have indicated a family's disgrace or fall in status. In 1663 Golitsyn was amongst the youths who accompanied Tsar Aleksei on a pilgrimage to the Monastery of St. Savva at Zvenigorod,[15] and in records of 1666 he is referred to as "coach attendant" (gosudarev voznitsa).[16] Such duties became commonplace during the reign of Tsar Aleksei Mihhailovich who constantly visited religious establishments in the Moscow region and also maintained a number of country estates where he frequently retired with a large retinue for hunting and falconry.

From about 1658 until his first recorded posting outside Moscow in 1676 Golitsyn spent his life in and around Moscow in attendance upon the tsar and his family. There is little here to distinguish Golitsyn from his contemporaries, indeed the period of "inactive" service may seem overly long. Golitsyn was in his thirties by the time he received his first important appointment, although there are hints that he may have been singled out earlier. In 1668, for example, he was a commander of the tsar's bodyguard -- glavnyi nad sotnikami vybornoi sotni.[17]

During his period of court service Golitsyn was married, seventeen or eighteen being the customary age. Some sources record a first marriage to one Fedos'ia Vasil'evna Dolgorukaia,[18] but it must have been very brief, for in 1663 Golitsyn's second wife Evdok'ia Ivanovna Streshneva gave birth to their first child, Irina, and in 1665 a son, Aleksei, was born.[19] Tereshchenko's suggestion that Streshneva was his first wife and Dolgorukaia his second is invalidated by copious evidence.[20] Other children of the marriage included a daughter Edvok'ia born in 1677 and possibly two sons, whose names are recorded in a Golitsyn genealogy of 1682 but missing from the lists in the Barkhatnaia kniga of 1687.[21] Another son, Mikhail, was born in 1689. From what we can gather from the meager sources available, Golitsyn had a happy family life, although, as will be shown later, his fidelity was called into question by his relationship with Tsarevna Sophia.

In 1675 Golitsyn, hitherto a faint image, begins to take on more substance. He himself supplied a laconic account of his service career from this date in a petition of 1684, which was later verified and supplemented by government enquiries.[23] In December 1675 he was ordered by Tsar Aleksei to go to the Ukraine with Prince K.O. Shcherbatov,[24] and in anticipation of this posting was made chief table attendant at the beginning of 1676.[25] On 29 January, Tsar Aleksei died and Golitsyn was amongst those raised to the rank of boyar by the new tsar Fedor immediately upon his accession.[26]

At the same time his appointment to the Ukraine was confirmed and he was charged with gathering information from Russian and Cossack officials. The prince's enhanced status was reflected in his prominence in the procession that accompanied Tsar Aleksei's coffin to the Kremlin Cathedral of the Archangel.[27]

On May 14 Golitsyn had a farewell audience with the tsar and a week or so later set out for the Ukraine, arriving in the military garrison of Sevsk on June 26.[28] It was, as far as we know, his first major trip away from the capital, Golitsyn arrived in the Ukraine at a time when political relations in the region were still tense and ambiguous. In 1653 the Cossack leader Bogdan Khmel'nitsky had sworn allegiance to the Tsar of Muscovy, who thus affirmed his ancestors' ancient claim to Little Russia. The annexation led to an extended war between Muscovy and Poland, its rival for suzereinty, which was concluded in 1667 by the Treaty of Andrusovo, which made the River Dniepr the boundary between Russian Left Bank and Polish Right Bank Ukraine, with Kiev and its environs ceded to Moscow for a temporary period of two years. The border was in many ways an artificial one, for the inhabitants of both sides had linguistic and religious ties, and a common enemy in the Crimean Tatars, who sporadically raided the area. In 1672 the uneasy balance of power was further disturbed by a Turkish-Tatar invasion of the Polish Ukraine, which forced Poland to cede part of the Right Bank to Turkey and to pay a large indemnity. Both Right and Left Banks had their separately appointed leader or hetman, Peter Dorofeevich Doroshenko (from 1666) and Ivan Samoilovich (from 1672) respectively, but the equilibrium had been upset in 1667 when Doroshenko rejected the Andrusovo terms and laid claim to jurisdiction over both sides. He swore allegiance to the Turks and attempts by the Poles to replace him by a more loyal appointee in 1674 ended in failure. Meanwhile Samoilovich also claimed the title of Hetman of Both Sides of the Dniepr, with the tacit backing of the Muscovite authorities, who had never ceased to regard the whole of the Ukraine as the tsar's patrimony.

Russia's tasks in the Ukraine were complex. Her civil and military officials were obliged to defend the area against Turkish and Tatar attacks, to ward of Polish encroachment, especially claims to Kiev, which had been retained beyond the two-year deadline, and to intervene in local disputes and rivalries amongst the independently-minded Cossack population. Golitsyn's brief appears to have been a comprehensive one; he was to receive and coordinate reports from local officials, including the commander-in-chief Prince G.G. Romodanovsky, his uncle Aleksei who was governor of Kiev, and from Hetman Samoilovich himself.[30] One of his first tasks, mentioned in the petition of 1684, was to settle a dispute between the hetman and Peter Roslavets, colonel of the Starodub regiment, who was refusing to recognise Samoilovich's authority. The case was decided in Samoilovich's favor.[31] Of greater significance was the capture in the autumn of 1676 of Doroshenko's Right Bank capital of Chigirin. The Russians dispatched a force of several thousand across the Dniepr, leaving Doroshenko little alternative but to submit and swear allegiance to the tsar.[32] The nature of Golitsyn's role in these manouevers remains obscure, but he was awarded the Turkish sultan's mace, part of the insignia of office confiscated from Doroshenko.[33] The prince's part in this and other operations was to be exaggerated after his rise to power, especially in the laudatory charter of 1684 which marked his services to the crown in 1676-78.[34] Although Doroshenko's change of allegiance strengthened Moscow's prestige in the short term, Russia derived little ultimate benefit from the capture of Chigirin, which two years later had to be abandoned in ruins. Russia's actions antagonised the Poles, in whose territory the town lay, and the Turks, to whom Doroshenko had turned for protection. In October 1676 a treaty between Poland and Turkey ceded possession of most of the Right Bank to the Turks.

One development of 1676, which acquired significance only in later years, may have been the beginning of cool relations between Golitsyn and Hetman Samoilovich. The award of part of his rival's insignia to the prince may have offended the hetman, but there seems to be no confirmation of the rumor that Samoilovich aroused the prince's displeasure by refusing to betroth his daughter to Golitsyn's son, who was only eleven years old at the time.[35]

The main excitement over, Golitsyn spent his last weeks in the region directing the construction of fortifications at the garrison of Putivl.[36] On September 23 he received orders from Moscow to take a count of the troops and return to the capital with a list for submission to the razriad, the chancellery of military affairs.[37] This he did, arriving back in the capital in late October-early November.[38]

1677 was to prove an even busier year. Back in Moscow at the end of 1676 Golitsyn was appointed director of the pushkarskii prikaz, the department which administered the artillery and the production of heavy weaponry and ammunition.[39] Another notable event is also recorded; on January 18 one of our most valuable contemporary witnesses, the Scottish mercenary Patrick Gordon, makes his first reference in his diary to a meeting with Golitsyn. It is recorded that the prince invited him to dinner, but Gordon was unable to accept owing to illness.[40] This evidence of Golitsyn's contact with foreigners some years before his appointment as foreign minister made this an integral part of his duties is valuable. It is an aspect of his activities to which reference will be made ever more frequently, for the prince's foreign acquaintances have left a much more vivid picture of him than any of his Russian contemporaries. A few years later he was to meet another of Peter I's future favorites, the Swiss soldier Franz Lefort, who wrote approvingly of Golitsyn in a letter to his brother.[41]

On March 12 Golitsyn received orders to return to the Ukraine with the same brief as in the previous year.[42] He took leave of the tsar on May 9 and on June 12 arrived in Sevsk, where he was met by Patrick Gordon's regiment.[43] The next day Gordon was able to take up the postponed invitation and dined with the prince, who expressed the wish to visit the Scot in his quarters. Gordon records that he entertained the prince as best he could.[44] Shortly afterwards Golitsyn transferred to the garrison at Putivl', where on July 23 he was instructed by a royal messenger to march to Pereiaslav and join up with Samoilovich and his troops in anticipation of a Turkish attack on the Right Bank and Chigirin.[45]

The Turks intended to take their revenge for the Muscovite incursion of the previous year. At the beginning of August a force of some 60,000 Turks, 40,000 Tatars and 19,000 Wallachians and Moldavians, accompanied by the latest Turkish-backed candidate for the hetmanship, Yury Khmel'nitsky, besieged the 12,000-strong garrison in Chigirin.[46] Golitsyn and his troops left Putivl' around August 7, receiving news of the seige shortly afterwards and numerous missives from Hetman Samoilovich advising him to change his route and make for Lubno rather than Pereiaslav.[47] As things turned out, the route was of little significance. Golitsyn's regiment of some 15-20,000 men seems to have acted in an auxilliary capacity and according to Gordon, who took part in the main action, the prince made camp on the Dniepr near Chigirin on August 29, after the main fighting was already over.[48] It is also reported that Golitsyn sent stores and two apothecaries to the town.[49] The main battles were fought by 20-25,000 Ukrainians under Samoilovich and 32,000 Russians under Romodanovsky who, on August 28-29, succeeded in putting the Turks and Tatars to flight and lifting the siege.

Accounts of the siege written after Golitsyn's rise to power afforded the prince a more distinguished role. In his 1684 petition he himself claimed: "Learning of the approach of the sovereign's men-at-arms and of all the regiments to the Dniepr, the vizier of the Turkish sultan, Abraim Seitan Pasha, fled from the Dniepr and Chigirin, having burnt his camp and abandoning many tents at Chigirin."[50] A decree issued in response to this confirmed: "And you, our boyar and commander, having heard of the approach of those Turkish forces and of the Crimean khan and his hordes, and that they had laid firm siege to Chigirin and continued to attack the town, you marched with your regiment of the sovereign's men-at-arms to the towns of Little Russia and to the Dniepr and Chigirin with great haste, and the Turkish pasha Ibrahim Sheitan and the Crimean khan and their troops, seeing the approach of your regiment of many men-at-arms, our boyar and commander, and of your fellow officers, retreated from the Dniepr and Chigirin and fled to the River Dunai, and the Crimean khan went with his horde into the Crimea."[51]

On September 12 the returning armies of Romodanovsky and Samoilovich reached Golitsyn's camp, but, reports Gordon, the two Russian commanders had a dispute over rank and did not meet; only the hetman visited the prince. "Although Gordon and many of the other officers would have liked to pay their respects to Prince Golitsyn, they did not dare inform their boyar [i.e. Romodanovsky] of this."[52] Such disputes were commonplace before the abolition of the Code of Precedence; no doubt Romodanovsky, as senior commanding officer in the Ukraine, was suspicious of his junior's special brief from Moscow. For his part, Golitsyn was later to refer to the large rewards received by Romodanovsky for the period 1676-81 when complaining of lack of recognition of his own services.[53]

On October 9 Golitsyn arrived back in Sevsk, and on October 11 was accompanied a short way by Gordon and other officers at the start of his journey back to Moscow.[54] Gordon's meeting with Golitsyn in 1677 must have convinced him that the prince was both a man of influence and a friend to foreigners, for it was to Golitsyn that he addressed a letter written in late October, asking him intercede with the tsar and obtain permission for Gordon to come to Moscow. The request was granted.[55]

News of Golitsyn's growing influence and a few all too rare personal details can be gleaned from a batch of letters which survive from the year 1677 from relatives, friends and subordinates. One correspondent begged the prince to intervene in the case of some runaway peasants;[56] his uncle Aleksei asks him to pay sympathetic attention to a member of his regiment;[57] his mother-in-law asks him to take under his wing one

11

Gavrilo Golovkin, "a young child", and to register him in his own unit, at the request of his grandmother, a nun.[58] One of his subordinates in the Artillery Chancellery reported on the production of new weapons and asked for his superior's intervention and advice in the case of drunken behavior by employees, unpaid wages and a clerk who was beating the apprentices. "And I beat my slavish brow on the ground beneath your feet," concludes the correspondent, in the conventional style of an inferior to a superior.[59]

Some of the letters kept Golitsyn informed of developments in Russia, no doubt at his own request. In a letter of July 5 one of his stewards, Ivan Divov, reported on affairs in the capital and on a terrible storm and fire in Tobolsk,[60] whilst on August 9 M. Boev informed Golitsyn of the exile of Ivan and Afanasy Naryshkin, brothers of the late tsar's second wife, who had fallen into disfavor as a result of the restored fortunes of the Miloslavsky clan.[61] His mother was a particularly informative writer. "My dear," she writes, "I reply to all your letters unceasingly and write about what I hear in town, which honors have been conferred on which people on which days by the sovereign, and who is in attendance."[62]

One of those "in attendance" was Golitsyn's son Aleksei. In a letter of July 14 the boy mentions his visits to court and the various breeds of horses that he had seen there.[63] Horseriding was evidently one of Aleksei's favorite pastimes and an essential accomplishment for young nobles at court. Service also involved expenses. On July 29 Aleksei informed his father that "the great sovereign has instructed his chamberlains (spal'niki) all to attend him with [blunt] weapons" and asked his father to send him one.[64] On July 23 Golitsyn's mother-in-law had reported that Aleksei was learning his lessons and that there was a good crop of red currants in the garden.[65]

These letters are particularly valuable for the glimpse they give of Golitsyn the family man. On August 2 his wife gave birth to a daughter and numerous friends and relatives hastened to inform him of the event and to offer their congratulations.[66] Golitsyn's reaction is not recorded. Female relatives showed anxiety for his health. On July 4 his mother-in-law wrote: "Rumors have reached us that you are in poor health,"[67] and on the same day his mother suggested that Vasily was probably suffering from the same complaint that had bothered his sister, "tightness and a heavy feeling in the chest, a bad cough, phlegm and a high fever." She offered to send him the doctor who had cured his sister.[68]

Finally we quote in full a letter from Golitsyn's

thirteen-year-old daughter Irina. Composed largly of
set formulae no doubt dictated by adults, it nevertheless gives some insight into family relations during
the period:

"To my father and lord Prince Vasily Vasil'evich,
your little daughter Oriutka begs your blessing and
pays you her humble respects. Be so good, my lord and
father, to write and inform me of your enduring health,
as God, my lord and father, may grant. Be so good, my
lord and father, to learn of the health of my lady
grandmother and lady mother and of my little brother
and me. My lady grandmother, Princess Tat'iana Ivanovna
and my lady mother Princess Avdot'ia Ivanovna and my
lord brother Prince Aleksei Vasil'evich and I are all
alive in Moscow this July 12 by God's grace and henceforth according to the will of our Lord and Creator. I
appeal to you, my lord and father, for my allowance for
soap. And I beg you, my lord and father, not to keep me
in suspense about your enduring health. Written by your
little daughter Oriutka, who begs your blessing and
pays you her humble respects."[69]

On July 23 Alesha and Irina sent a pound of
almonds and begged their father to eat them "for his
good health."[70]

In April 1678 Golitsyn again left his family for
the Ukraine, arriving in Sevsk in early May, where he
received a congratulatory rescript from the tsar prai-
sing him for his "speedy arrival."[71] He was told to
proceed to Putivl' and await further developments
there. At this point we lose track of Golitsyn's activities. "Further developments" did indeed take place,
with an attack by a huge army of Turks and Tatars upon
poorly defended Chigirin early in July. On August 3
Patrick Gordon took over from the garrison commander
Ivan Rzhevsky, who had been killed by an enemy shell,
but neither Gordon or other sources record Golitsyn's
presence during the campaign. Eventually Chigirin was
destroyed and abandoned after heavy losses on both
sides.[72] Gordon is not the only source to maintain an
intriguing silence on Golitsyn's activites in 1678-79.
Golitsyn himself omitted this period in his petition of
1684, suggesting that he was absent from active service
in the Ukraine.[73] The charter subsequently awarded to
him mentions payment for services rendered in the years
7184, 185, 188 and 189.[74] There is no hint of disgrace,
for on May 18, 1679 it is recorded that Golitsyn was
"first judge" in the Vladimir prikaz, or high court.[75]
This was an important post, and there are grounds for
believing that Golitsyn may have influenced some of the
minor legal reforms introduced at the end of Fedor's
reign. He appears to have remained in Moscow that year;
on August 15 he dined at the patriarch's table and on

August 19 attended the tsar at a liturgy in the Kremlin and then accompanied him to the royal estate at Kolomenskoe. Golitsyn's name appears at the head of a list of servitors who attended the tsar, a further confirmation that his status was in no way diminished.[76]

In 1680 Golitsyn resumed his service in the Ukraine. There were no large-scale military operations that year as peace negotiations with the Turks and Tatars were in progress, but the 1684 petition claims that Golitsyn's arrival in the region again "intimidated" the sultan and khan.[77] From late 1679 new defence lines were being constructed in the area and old ones renovated, and Golitsyn was again instructed to carry out repairs on the fortifications at Putivl'.[78] In July he took part in reconnaissance manouevers and was instructed to broadcast news of the tsar's marriage to Agaf'ia Grushetskaia.[79] Golitsyn arrived back in Moscow at the end of August to be confronted with a personal loss. As he records: "By the will of God, at the beginning of August my wretched Moscow dwelling burnt down and many of my miserable possessions were lost in the flames."[80] We have no further details of the incident, but shortly afterwards Golitsyn began to construct a fine mansion in the center of Moscow, which later commanded the admiration of foreigners and Muscovites alike.

Golitsyn's stay in Moscow was brief, for in November he was sent back to the Ukraine as commander-in-chief of the Sevsk military district, a post which he held until August 1681.[81] The signing of the Treaty of Bakhchisarai with Turkey and the Crimea in January 1681 allowed for a more relaxed atmosphere.[82] Golitsyn continued to organise troop movements and fortification building and to attend to local matters, including the recovery of fugitive soldiers.[83] He did not take direct part in the peace negotiations, but was later commended for the fact that he was serving in Sevsk at the time of the agreement, another example of the way in which Golitsyn's by no means dishonorable record prior to his rise to the helm of government was sometimes artificially boosted.

Golitsyn returned to Moscow in August 1681[85] and was do not return to the south until the first ill-fated Crimean campaign some six years later. In the capital one of the most significant undertakings of his career awaited him, for in November he was appointed to head a commission to review Russia's military organisation. No doubt the prince's record in the Ukraine had impressed Fedor and his advisers, and it has also been suggested that he may have participated in previous military and fiscal reforms implemented by Fedor's regime in the period 1678-81.[86] These included the

14

introduction of a unified tax for the maintenance of the musketeers, the creation of new military districts and the establishment of regular units of infantry and cavalry.

On January 12 1682 the boyar council, hierarchs of the Church and representatives of other classes of the Muscovite state gathered in the presence of the tsar and patriarch to hear the commission's recommendations.[87] In its report, delivered by Golitsyn himself, the commission proposed that the essential preliminary to any military reform was the abolition of the Code of Precedence (mestnichestvo), the system whereby military and civic appointments were made on the basis of a candidate's pedigree and his family's service record. It proposed that all military servitors should be assigned to commissions without regard to procedence (chtoby byli mezhdu soboi bez mest). Such a move was not unheralded; the power of the old aristocracy had been weakened during the Time of Troubles at the beginning of the century, and since then a number of men of low birth had risen to high civic office. This was especially true of the circle of advisers around the throne -- blizhnie liudi -- who relied upon the monarch's personal favor for promotion. On many occasions prior to 1682 the code had been temporarily suspended during major campaigns and for lesser events. One of the incidents reported to Golitsyn in letters of 1677, for example, was that the tsar had held a banquet "without regard to precedence."[88] Despite such concessions the code continued to hamper Russia's efficiency in warfare, causing constant disputes about seniority which Golitsyn himself must have experienced frequently whilst on service in the Ukraine. The inadequacy of the old system was shown up even more vividly by the use of new military formations and foreign units.

The commission's recommendations were favorably received by the tsar and patriarch, the former declaring the code to be the cause of "great misfortune in war, diplomacy and other affairs of state." The registers of precedence were solemnly burned to the words: "May this Code, hateful to God, creative of enmity, hateful to brotherhood and destructive of love perish in the flames and nevermore be recalled for all time."[89]

The abolition of the Code of Precedence was a significant event in Golitsyn's career, showing him to be a champion of at least a limited degree of meritocracy, despite the advantages which he himself enjoyed under the old system. The measure hastened the amalgamation of the Muscovite hereditary and service nobility into one undifferentiated class and was an important precursor of Peter I's Table of Ranks (1722). The abo-

lition was probably the most, and also the last significant measure of Fedor's short reign. In July 1681 his
wife Agaf'ia and her new-born son died shortly after
her confinement.[90] Despite the tsar's own failing
health, on February 15 1682 a second marriage, to
fifteen-year-old Martha Matveevna Apraksina, took place
without any of the usual festivities in what was evidently a desperate attempt to continue the dynasty.[91]
On April 27, however, at the age of 21 Fedor died,
leaving no direct heir. His death plunged Russia into a
tangled dynastic crisis.

# CHAPTER TWO

## THE MUSKETEER REBELLION OF 1682

The troubles which broke out after Fedor's death brought to the surface not only the rivalries of the factions around the throne but also the perennial grievances of Moscow's military forces, the peasantry and townspeople and religious dissenters. The heir apparent was Fedor's sixteen-year-old brother Ivan, Aleksei's only surviving son by his first wife Maria Miloslavskaia. Ivan was by all accounts a kindly and pious soul, but he suffered from both physical and mental disorders, including a disease of the eyes and a speech impediment. It was evident that he could never be more than a token ruler. His ten-year-old half brother Peter, on the other hand, the offspring of Tsar Aleksei's second marriage, to Natalia Naryshkina, was healthy and intelligent, and could be expected to function as an independant monarch upon reaching maturity. The striking contrast between the two brothers was remarked upon by a foreign visitor who saw them in July 1683:

"The elder tsar sat motionless and with downcast gaze, his eyes half covered with a cap pulled down over them. The younger, his face uplifted and uncovered, allowed his marvellous beauty to shine forth with agreeable gestures, whilst his face was shot through with the crimson of his blood... If he had been a young woman and not a royal personage, all those around would have fallen in love with him."[1]

J.E. Hövel, secretary to a Swedish delegation which visited Moscow in February 1683, reported that Ivan was "a very sick, lame, blind gentleman, with a growth of skin right over his eyes."[2]

Had Ivan and Peter been full brothers it is likely that the succession could have been decided in Peter's favor without serious repercussions; but the boys represented the hopes of rival factions based on the relatives of their respective mothers. As it turned out, Patriarch Joachim initiated the election of Peter as the new monarch on the day of Fedor's death and the decision was ratified by a hastily convoked zemskii sobor.[3] The move did not long remain unchallenged. During Fedor's funeral on April 28 the first protests were voiced by the Miloslavsky circle. Flouting the convention which prevented the daughters of the tsar from participating openly in public ceremonies, Ivan and Fedor's sister Sophia followed the coffin to the Cathedral of the Archangel and later denounced Tsaritsa Natalia, who left before the end of the service taking

Peter with her. Sophia attracted the attention of the crowds with her loud wailing, hinting that her brother's death had been precipitated by poison and complaining that Ivan had been robbed of his inheritance:

"See how our brother Fedor unexpectedly departed this world, poisoned by his ill-wishers. Pity us poor orphans -- we have neither father, mother nor brother. Our elder brother Ivan has not been chosen to sit on the throne. If we have offended you or the boyars, allow us to go alive to some foreign land and Christian monarch."[3]

The seeds of doubt were sown. Apart from the not unjustified claim that Ivan had been usurped, in the days that followed Sophia and her supporters were able to cast other aspersions upon the integrity of Peter's party, some well-founded, like complaints about the undeserved honors and promotions heaped upon the Naryshkins on April 27, others, such as charges of attempted regicide, treason and defilation of royal regalia, fabricated or exaggerated.

How is perhaps the moment to look more closely at the 25-year-old woman who emerged as spokesman for the Miloslavsky faction and to whom Golitsyn's own fate was to be so intimately bound. At the time of Fedor's death there were six daughters surviving from Tsar Aleksei's first marriage and one from his second.[5] Two of Tsar Mikhail Fedorovich's daughters, Tat'iana and Anna, were still alive, and the two dowager Tsaritsas Natalia and Martha completed the formidable contingent of royal females. Before the reforms of the Petrine era the daughters of the Muscovite tsars generally came to public attention only through announcements of their births and deaths. They had little to expect from life. Even the role of political pawns enjoyed by their counterparts in the West was denied them owing to the sanctions upon marriage with foreigners of different faith; and the undesirablity of marrying "below" them into the Russian nobility placed them almost wholly beyond the matrimonial pale. They were confined to the women's quarters--terem--of the palace, with occasional outings to church or sometimes further afield to religious establishments in the Moscow region. They were not obliged to take the veil, as has sometimes been suggested, but they lived lives scarcely less secluded than that of a nun.[6] During Tsar Aleksei's reign, however, the picture began to change. As S.M. Solov'ev wrote, new customs and views began to penetrate the court, "the doors of the tsarevnas' terem had opened wide and the captives had seen the light of day."[7] Sophia, for example, was educated by her brothers' tutor, the Belorussian churchman and writer Simeon Polotsky, who dedicated his work The Crown of Faith to her. Perhaps

18

equally important, after Tsar Aleksei's death the absence of a strong male figure in the palace gave the women the opportunity for more self-assertion. A Polish witness to the events of 1682 reported, for example, that Tsarevna Ekaterina had discarded the traditional caftan in favor of Polish dress and no longer wore her hair in a plait.[8] Sophia's dramatic appearance in public at her brother's funeral was not, then, entirely unheralded.

Although some later writers were to refer to Sophia as a "handsome young lady",[9] contemporaries either make no reference to her appearance or, in at least one case, pronounced her to be ugly. In a much quoted passage the Frenchman De la Neuville wrote:

"The Princess Sophia, whose wit and capability in no way resembled the difformity of her body, was monstrously fat, with a head as big as a bushel, a hairy face and carbuncles on her legs, and was at least forty years old."[10] Another contemporary witness, Georg Schleissing from Saxony, wrote that "the shape of her body was not at all beautiful, but nevertheless she was a very clever princess, endowed with noble qualities of mind."[11] His book contains a not very flattering full-length portrait of Sophia in profile.

Both writers felt obliged to qualify their remarks about Sophia's appearance by reference to her intellect. As De la Neuville went on to say, "just as her figure is broad, short and gross, so her intellect is fine, subtle and shrewd, and without ever having read Machiavelli, she has a natural command of all his maxims, above all that there is nothing which may not be undertaken and no crime which may not be committed when ruling is at stake."[12] Voltaire was later to write (without reference to De la Neuville's remarks on Sophia's appearance): "She was possessed of a great share of understanding and some wit, made verses in the Russian language, and both wrote and spoke extremely well. These talents were set off by the addition of an agreeable person and sullied only by her ambition."[13]

Sophia's ambition is the trait on which all writers are agreed, although not all are united in condemning it. Peter I is alleged to have stated that she was "endowed with all the Accomplishments of Body and Mind to Perfection, had it not been for her boundless Ambition and insatiable Desire for governing."[14] Catherine II, a ruler perhaps even more ambitious than Sophia, wrote, on the other hand: "A great deal has been said about this princess; but I do not think that in general authors have done her justice."[15]

Most surviving assessments of Sophia date from the end of her regency or later, after the "official" version of her lust for power and determination to extend her rule beyond Peter's coming of age was well established. There is little direct evidence to elucidate Sophia's state of mind in April/May 1682 or to suggest that at this stage she looked any further than safegarding Ivan's claim to the throne and thus limiting the authority of the Naryshkin clan, from whom the Miloslavsky princesses could expect little sympathy.

There is even less evidence to determine Golitsyn's attitude. It has been suggested that even before Fedor's death he had instigated a "plot", urging Sophia to show special solicitude to the dying tsar and seek power after his death.[16] Ustrialov maintains that it was precisely during Fedor's last illness, when magnates attended the tsar in his sickroom to conduct urgent business, that a meeting first took place between Sophia and her future minister.[17] These rumors would appear to originate with De la Neuville, who writes that Sophia, "being unable to succeed in her grand design without large support, began to form a party and, having examined those around her, decided that Prince Golitsyn was the most capable of leading it."[18] Of all the nobles who attended the tsar in 1681-82, Golitsyn could not have failed to impress the astute Sophia as one of the most talented, especially in view of his recent prominence in the abolition of the Code of Precedences. Rumor and speculation apart, however, we have no precise information about the nature of the relationship between the pair at the time of Fedor's death. The appointment of Golitsyn's son Aleksei as a chamberlain in Peter's entourage on April 28[19] indicates that the new Naryshkin government saw no grounds for doubting Golitsyn's loyalty, nor did any of Golitsyn's own statements or actions in 1682 show overt hostility to Peter.

Practically the only documentary glimpses we catch of the prince in the days leading up to the rebellion of May 15 is his performance of ceremonial duties at Fedor's tomb on May 4, when he kept vigil in the company of ten lesser officials.[20] In the meantime Sophia and her party were making progress in harnessing the support of the Moscow garrison of musketeers, much as the guards regiments were to be utilised by aspiring rulers in the eighteenth century. The musketeers (strel'tsy), of whom there were nineteen regiments stationed in the capital, combined active military service and peacetime activities as guards, night watchmen and ceremonial attendants with their own private occupations as petty traders and craftsmen. The corps was administered by a government department, the streletskii prikaz. During Fedor's reign complaints had been made by rank and file musketeers about such issues as non-payments of allowances, loss of privileges, and abuse and interference from officers. These had largely been ignored and just four days before Fedor's death a musketeer had been sentenced to a beating for submitting a complaint against his superiors, but was rescued at the last minute by his comrades. Sixteen regiments subsequently submitted petitions against their officers and the dispute was still unresolved when Fedor died.[21] The corps took the oath of allegiance to Peter, no doubt in anticipation of a resolution of their difficulties, but they did not stop complaining. The Naryshkin government was sufficiently intimidated by a petition of April 30 to charge several musketeer colonels with abusing their men and to sentence them to be beaten.[22] The musketeers were not appeased, however. There remained, amongst other things, the issue of back pay and the universal hatred with which the directors of the streletskii prikaz Prince Yu.A. Dolgoruky and his son Mikhail were regarded by their men.

A number of ploys seem to have been used by the Miloslavsky faction in order to win the allegiance of the musketeers and turn their discontnent against the new regime. These included direct negotiation with the more militant rank-and-file, the distribution of bribes and the dissemination of rumors, although as events were to prove, the musketeers were a restive force over whom even Sophia's party was quickly to lose control. The rumors ranged from allegations that the boyars, almost all of whom supported Peter, were preparing to punish the musketeers for their insubordination to claims that Natalia Naryshkina's 23-year-old brother Ivan had tried on royal regalia, sat on the throne and even tried to strangle Tsarevich Ivan. The musketeers had no good reason to favor either the Naryshkins of the Miloslavskys, so it was essential for the latter to play upon the credulity of the corps and its belief in the "true tsar" by dispelling the idea that Peter's election had been a sane and practical measure and suggesting instead that it had been engineered by the cunning of the power-loving Naryshkins, who were hostile to the musketeers and would stop at nothing, not even the murder of the "rightful heir" Ivan, in order to secure their "puppet's" rule. It was the rumor of regicide that brought the musketeers to the Kremlin on May 15, a day already heavy with associations, being the anniversary of the alleged murder, in 1591, of Ivan IV's son Dmitry.

The dramatic events which followed have been well chronicled, although there are many discrepancies in surviving accounts. In short, around noon regiments began to march to the Kremlin in order to seek out the "murderers" of Tsarevich Ivan. Some reports suggest that their leaders had been supplied with a list of "traitors", pre-selected by the Miloslavsky ring-leaders, against whom they were to vent their wrath. Upon arrival in the Kremlin the musketeers were momentarily stopped in their tracks by the sight of Ivan himself, who was brought out onto a balcony to quash any rumors of his death. Some of the boyars tried to negotiate with the rebels, urging them to return to their homes, and Artamon Matveev, Tsar Aleksei's former foreign minister, only recently recalled from exile by the Naryshkin government, is said to have delivered a speech promising to intercede on the musketeers' behalf. Unfortunately these conciliatory efforts were undermined by Prince Mikhail Dolgoruky, the deputy director of the musketeer chancellery, who began shouting at his men. He was attacked and cut to pieces by a section of the crowd, which then proceeded to rampage through the Kremlin.

Dolgoruky's murder marked the beginning of a massacre that claimed many distinguished victims, includng Prince Yury Dolgoruky, Artamon Matveev, several Naryshkins and Golitsyn's old rival Prince G.G. Romodanovsky. On May 16 the musketeers returned to the Kremlin to demand that Tsaritsa Natalia's brother Ivan be handed over to them. Despite efforts to save him, on the following day he was tortured and killed. Another victim of that day was the foreign doctor Daniel von Gaden, whom the mob accused of practising sorcery and administering poison to Tsar Fedor. In the days that followed the insurgents were able to elicit further concessions from the intimidated government, including the banishment of Tsaritsa Natalia's father Kirill Naryshkin, the exile of other Nayrshkins and favorites of the previous regime and promises of thousands of rubles' worth of unpaid allowances and additional bonus payments.

This account of the events of May 15-17 has been kept deliberately brief for the reason that Golitsyn figures very insignificantly. Only one known contemporary version records his presence at the rebellion, an official chronology entitled "smutnoe vremia" and probably dating from the end of 1682,[23] which records that on May 15 a small group of boyars, including Prince V.V. Golitsyn, Prince M.A. Cherkassky, Prince I.A. Khovansky and P.V. Sheremet'ev, were sent out to pacify the musketeers when they first arrived in the Kremlin. One may suppose that when the mob errupted Golitsyn made his escape along with other courtiers and officials; there are no explicit references to his being at the side of Sophia and the royal party in the Kremlin during the events that ensued. Of course, Golitsyn's apparently prudent absence from the scene of the massacres does not absolve him of charges of participating in the plot which led up to the rebellion but, curiously, contemporary witnesses are silent on this point, too. Andrei Artamonovich Matveev, son of the murdered boyar, for example, who was present throughout the rebellion, singles out Ivan Mikhailovich Miloslavsky as the ringleader of the conspiracy and fails to mention Golitsyn amongst the accomplices.[24] Matveev was a member of the Naryshkin circle and had no reason to be sympathetic towards Golitsyn. Later in his account of Sophia's regency, he confirms that "at that time the boyar Prince Vasily Vasil'evich Golitsyn enjoyed the tsarevna's most extensive favor," but singles out the "other favorite" Fedor Shaklovity as predominant in the plotting and scheming which culminated in Sophia's downfall in 1689.[25] Neither does Silvester Medvedev, who admittedly was a member of Sophia's party, make any reference to the prince's role; in fact, in one edition of his account of the rebellion of 1682 the editor saw fit to supplement this omission with a footnote to the effect that Ivan Miloslavsky and Golitsyn were the chief conspirators.[26] The short account by a Polish eye-witness also omits to mention the prince.[27]

The case against Golitsyn remains unproven. In general one can endorse the verdicts of other historians assessing the same materials, who concluded that Golitsyn was "completely unfitted for the role of conspirator" and "abhorred violence and despised intrigue."[28] "Decisive, criminal acts" were not his forte.[29] This verdict is strengthened by our knowledge of Golitsyn's indecisiveness in August–September 1689, when he also seems to have failed to participate directly in Sophia's attemps to use the musketeers against Peter.

On May 16 a list of government appointments was issued, allocating the Foreign Office or Ambassadorial Chancellery (posol'skii prikaz) to Golitsyn, with State Secretary Emel'ian Ukraintsev as his deputy.[30] Other appointments included Prince Ivan Andreevich Khovansky as director of the Musketeers' Chancellery and Ivan Miloslavsky to the Foreigners', Cavalry and Artillery Chancelleries. That Golitsyn's appointment was soon common knowledge is confirmed by the Danish resident Butenant, who reported that on May 17 he asked Golitsyn, to whom the Foreign Office had been transferred in the stead of a State Secretary Larion Ivanov to provide a guard for his protection, which was supplied the next day.[31]

There is no reason to jump to the conclusion that Golitsyn's elevation to high office was merely a "reward" for his part in Sophia's scheme. It should be borne in mind that on May 16 the troubles were still unresolved and Peter was, at least nominally, still tsar. Even if some of the new appointment reflect Sophia's growing influence, the inclusion of a number of boyars in the list, a group which in general supported Peter, showed that the Miloslavskys could not function without the cooperation of the high-ranking nobles who customarily headed government departments. Golitsyn was well qualified to become foreign minister even without Sophia's backing. Equally, it would be wrong to dismiss Sophia's patronage altogether. Prince B.I. Kurakin firmly attributed Golitsyn's rise to power to "the special inclination and amour" of Sophia. He had won favor through "amorous intrigue" but, Kurakin adds, he was "handsome in his person, of great intellect and loved by all."[32] De la Neuville also suggests that Golitsyn's appointment was not viewed with any immediate hostility: "As he was a man of great quality, indisputably descended from the last Duke of Lithuania, from the house of Jagellon, the nobles were at first satisfied with this choice, persuading themselves that he would be Minister only in name, and that they would share all authority with him. But the prince, who had more wit than the whole of Muscovy put together, did not care to sustain them in their expectations."[33] In this passage De la Neuville writes with hindsight of Golitsyn's eminence at the end of Sophia's regency; in May 1682 he was still only a chancellery director, albeit of one of the most important government departments. Other more comprehensive honors were heaped upon him only later, including the imposing title "Guardian of the great royal seal and the state's great ambassadorial affairs," which was authorised for use in communications with foreign powers on October 19, 1682:[34]

"The great sovereigns have decreed that the privy councillor and prefect of Novgorod Prince Vasily Vasil'evich Golitsyn, when in communication with the ambassadors and envoys of neighboring sovereigns, and in letters of reply and important communications with Ivan Samoilovich, Hetman of the Zaporozhian Host of Both Sides of the Dniepr, shall call himself Guardian of the great royal seal and the state's great ambassadorial affairs."[35] Even then the title seems to have been restricted to diplomatic usage and Golitsyn is not referred to consistently as guardian (oberegatel') until later in the regency. Not until September 1685, for example, was the title sanctioned for inclusion in the register of boyars.[36]

The musketeer rebellion, then, had allowed the Miloslavskys to undermine their main opponents and to appoint a number of sympathisers to high office, but as yet no constitutional change had been effected. Peter, although deprived of the leading lights of his mother's party, was still sole ruler. The next step towards the legalisation of Sophia's power came on May 23, when a petition from the musketeers, no doubt prompted from above, requested that Ivan rule jointly with his brother. This resolution was accepted by an assembly of churchmen, boyars and townspeople, who on May 26 acceded to another request by the musketeers that Ivan be recognised as "senior" tsar.[37] On May 29 Sophia Alekseevna was appointed regent for the duration of her brothers' minority. It is significant that from the outset Sophia coupled her name with that of her brothers "for the complete establishment of the administration of the state and for firm continuity in all affairs." A decree of May 29 proposed the following multiple formulae for royal rescripts:   "The great sovereigns, tsars and grand princes Ivan Alekseevich and Peter Alekseevich, autocrats of all the Great and Little and White Russias and their sister the great sovereign lady, noble tsarevna and grand princess Sophia Alekseevna...have decreed and the boyars have resolved."[38]

The musketeers, however, with whose aid the new regime had been established, were not content to step meekly out of the limelight now that the Miloslavskys had attained their ends. In the aftermath of the rebellion they demanded back pay since 1646 and the banishment of some of the leading figures of the previous reign. The name of the corps was changed to "household infantry" (nadvornaia pekhota). The Musketeer Chancellery was now headed by Prince Ivan Khovansky, nicknamed the "Braggart", who seized upon the chance to further his own ambitions through the corps. Sophia's government was forced to accede to a number of demands, including an undertaking that no blame or disapproval should be attached to the musketeers' activities of May 15-17. On June 6, moreover, the musketeers submitted a list of those killed during the riot with reasons for their executions, and demanded that a column be raised on Red Square to commemorate the musketeers' heroic feats and inscribed with the names of the "traitors".[39] It is interesting that in their petitions the musketeers mentioned as sympathisers other sections of the Moscow populace who had taken little part in the rebellion, including the artillery men, tradespeople and artisans. During the troubles the premises of the slavery Chancellery were ransacked and certificates of bondage destroyed, apparently in an effort to make the slaves claim their freedom. It is doubtful, however, whether this apparent attempt to widen the democratic significance of the rebellion was anything more than an attempt by the musketeers to gain moral support against possible retaliation by the authorities.

Unfortunately we have no record of Golitsyn's

25

attitude towards the relations between the musketeers and the new regime. His foreign office duties did not involve him in direct dealing with the corps and what we know of the prince's own interests and apparent distaste for intrigue makes it likely that he spent the last days of May and early weeks of July acquainting himself with his new office, whilst leaving others to deal with the musketeers.

One of the events in which Golitsyn did take a leading role was the novel dual coronation of the new tsars on June 25. It was necessary to manufacture additional sets of regalia, robes and a throne for the "junior" tsar Peter and arrangements for the lavish ceremonials were made by Golitsyn's deputy Ukraintsev under the prince's supervision.[40] The prince's low profile during the May events did not prevent him from emerging now as the most prominent courtier in a society which despite the abolition of the Code of Precedence still set great store by the hierarchy of personnel at processions, receptions and banquets. Several accounts of the coronation survive, with some discrepancies of detail.[41] All are agreed that Golitsyn headed the group of boyars sent by the tsars in the early morning to fetch crosses, shoulder mantles, crowns and scepters from the Treasury. He accompanied the regalia to the cathedral, then returned to inform the tsars that everything was ready for their investiture. During the ceremony, according to some accounts, Golitsyn stood with other selected officials, including the tsars' personal attendants, on the coronation dai and held the scepters during the liturgy.[42] If Sophia again louted convention and attended the ceremony openly, there is no record of it.

The tsars were safe y crowned, but the problem of the musketeers remained and was now further complicated by attempts by religious dissidents, strongly supported by Prince Ivan Khovansky, to gain influence through the corps, which already contained a significant Old Believer element. After abortive attempts to prevent the new tsars being crowned in the "Latin" rite, on July 5 a confrontation took place between dissidents' and representatives of the official Church in the Kremlin Palace of Facets, with Sophia herself presiding and displaying great public presence, courage and firmness.[43] Whether Golitsyn was present is not recorded, but there is reason to believe that he was in full sympathy with Sophia's denunciation of the dissidents' cause. On this occasion the musketeers eventually sided with the government and turned against the discredited Old Believer leaders, but on July 12 they again showed their sensitivity about possible retaliation by responding to rumors that the boyars wished to "extermi-

26

nate" them with demands that they be given custody of
all the boyars. Shortly after this incident, Sophia,
the tsars and much of the court left for the Trinity-
St. Sergius Monastery, leaving behind a committee of
boyars headed by Khovansky. This may have seemed like a
blunder at the time, for Khovansky and his son had
gained a strong hold over the musketeers and seemed
capable of turning them against the new regime. It was
Khovansky who had urged the musketeers to defend the
Old Belief and encouraged them to believe the rumors
about a boyar "plot". Rumors were now rife that Khovansky was seeking the crown, that he intended to kill the
tsars and the patriarch and restore the Old Belief. As
it turned out, however, whether by luck or by judge-
ment, the withdrawal of the court from Moscow succeeded
in undermining Khovansky's position.

Golitsyn accompanied the court on its July excur-
sion, but did not neglect his Foreign Office work. In
addition to the standard business of foreign affairs
and diplomacy, the chancellery had jurisdiction over a
number of subsidiary departments, including the
Vladimir, Galich, Little Russian, Novogorod, Smolensk
and Ustiug prikazy and also over several large monasteries. In December 1682 Golitsyn was also to take
charge of the Foreign Mercenaries (inozemskii) and
Cavalry (reitarskii) chancelleries.44 The wide variety
of business is reflected in correspondence between
Golitsyn and his deputy Ukraintsev during the month of
July. He reminded Ukraintsev to send off tribute payments to the Crimea, informed him of the tasks to be
allocated to chancellery officials and instructed him
on the transfer of funds (a common device of Muscovite
bookkeeping) from one department to another.45 He
promised to investigate complaints about the ineffi-
ciency of the iamskoi prikaz, the transport department
which, among other things, provided carriages and
horses for government officials. On July 26 Ukraintsev
informed his superior that falcon handlers due to
arrive in Moscow with new birds for the royal hawkery
had failed to appear and that the royal collection was
now reduced to twelve gerfalcons, all wild and untrain-
ed (of which one was sick and another had half a claw
missing), two old hawks and six young ones. Golitsyn
ordered Ukraintsev to try to obtain more birds.46

After a brief return to the capital, on August 20
the court again prepared to leave, this time for the
royal estate at Kolomenskoe to the south of Moscow.47
On September 1, with the court absent, the Muscovite
New Year was celebrated without the usual festivities,
which apparently cast a cloud of gloom over those who
remained in the city, including the musketeers. On
September 2 the court moved on to the Monastry of St.

Savva at Zvenigorod and that same day the first step towards the resolution of the Khovansky affair was taken with the discovery of an anonymous letter, allegedly written by a musketeer and two townsmen, revealing a plot by the Khovanskys to seize the throne, kill the tsars, Tsaritsa Natalia, Sophia, the patriarch and the boyars (including three unspecified Golitsyns) and restore the Old Belief.[48] This letter later formed part of the evidence against the Khovanskys. The court continued its "pilgrimage", stopping at a number of estates. Golitsyn had a personal annoyance to bear, for on September 8 it was reported that some of his servants, returning from a feast day celebration in a Moscow suburb, had been waylaid and assaulted. One of them was interrogated in the Musketeers Chancellery, then questioned personally by Prince Ivan Khovansky. In an appeal to the tsars, Golitsyn complained that his men were being victimised because of hostility between himself and Khovansky's son Andrei. He alleged that a musketeer unit had been sent to his house to collect the injured servants and had intimidated his entire household. He requested that the case be transferred to a more dispassionate judge and on September 11 it was taken over by the Siberian Chancellery.[49]

It was not unusual for bondsmen and servants to suffer vicariously as a result of their masters' feuds and disputes and although it may be tempting to see this incident as evidence of Golitsyn's concern for his underlings, it is likely that his own honor and reputation were of prime importance when he protested against the victimisation of his servants.

On September 13 the court arrived at the village of Vozdvizhenskoe, where Sophia issued a rescript summoning all state servitors, from boyars to minor gentry, to attend the tsars there by September 18. When it was reported that the Khovanskys had obeyed the summons and were on their way charges against them were made public; they has "committed various acts without the great sovereigns' permission, acting wilfully and opposing the great sovereigns' command in everything."[50] The anonymous letter was quoted. Fedor Shaklovity, a man by all accounts passionately devoted to Sophia, was appointed to head the Musketeer Chancellery and on September 17 Ivan and Andrei Khovansky were arrested and summarily executed. The next day Golitsyn was given the title of "household commander" and placed in charge of preparations for an anticipated musketeer backlash. The court moved to the Trinity-St. Sergius Monastery to prepare for a siege. Golitsyn's appointment remained an honorary one for no clash occurred, despite attempts by musketeers to seize weapons and ensconce themselves in the Kremlin. They were intimidated by the execution of

the man they had called their "father" and by rumors of
the punishments the government had in store for them.
On September 19 the musketeers went to the patriarch to
protest their innocence and lack of all "evil intentions", and begged the court to return. Over the next
two weeks a series of rescripts and petitions passed
between the Trinity Monastery and Moscow. On September
24 musketeer representatives came to the monastery to
submit a statement of their innocence; they had "no
evil intentions whatsoever against Their Majesties the
tsars, the boyars or the privy councillors either now
or henceforth."[51] On September 28 rescripts were sent
from the Trinity Monastery listing the conditions under
which a pardon would be granted:  the musketeers were
to desist from all riotous and rebellious assemblies,
to cease making petitions and to obey the orders of
their superiors unquestioningly.[52] On October 8 they
swore an oath of obedience before the patriarch in the
Cathedral of the Assumption, and on October 28, at
their own request, the column commemorating their
exploits was removed from Red Square. The "services" of
May 15-17 were now recognised as crimes.[53]

In the meantime Sophia hastened to reward all
those who had rallied to her support during the "Trinity campaign". On October 25 supplementary payments were
made to loyal state officials and military servitors,
the largest, 150 rubles, going to Golitsyn, who also
received 300 chets of land transferred from service to
hereditary tenure. Others received sums in the range of
40-100 rubles according to rank.[54] On October 27 the
court set out for Moscow and entered the city in procession on November 3, Golitsyn riding directly behind
the tsars. A service of thanksgiving was conducted by
the patriarch.

The triumphant entry into Moscow signalled victory
for Sophia and her party and a return to comparative
normality. The musketeers were cowed, the Naryshkin
faction decimated, with Tsaritsa Natalia relegated to
the background, and neither Ivan, permanently incapaci-
tated, nor Peter, as yet a boy, set any limitations on
the power of the regime. Even so, proclamations sent
abroad to announce the new joint reign as yet gave
little indication of the real power behind the thrones
of Tsars Ivan Alekseevich and Peter Alekseevich.[55]
Sophia had a number of talented supporters, foremost
amongst them Prince Vasily Golitsyn. The trust placed
in him by his appointment to the Foreign Office had
been reconfirmed by his nominal appointment as "household commander" and by the prominence allowed him on
state occasions, but Golitsyn was still to prove himself. There had been neither time nor opportunity to
carry out any important work in the Foreign Office; one

is struck, rather, by the mundane nature of many of the routine matters which were submitted for the minister's scrutiny and approval. In the midst of the Khovansky crisis, for example, Golitsyn received a memorandum from the tsars commanding him in his capacity as head of the Novgorod prikaz to arrange the transport of 40 barrels of fish.[56] More challenging tasks were soon to present themselves.

# CHAPTER THREE

## IN THE FOREIGN OFFICE

Sophia's regime was now generally recognised, but the troubles of 1682 required an extensive clearing-up operation. In December of that year a number of musketeer units were transferred from Moscow to Kiev, Smolensk, Astrakhan, Pskov and other border areas "as a safeguard against the unreliability of the musketeers and to guard against further unruliness."[1] As late as May 1683 the government had to issue a warning to those who continued to indulge in rumor and speculation about the mutiny.[2] The perennial problem of fugitive serfs, which had been exacerbated by the rebellion, was tackled in a series of enactments of 1682-83, most of which merely quoted the relevant passages from the Law Code of 1649.[3] Some historians, such as Ustrialov, view the whole seven years of Sophia's regency as a mere stopgap, a period of defensive government lacking in any broad vision of reform or consistent policies to improve the country's welfare.[4] S.M. Solov'ev, on the other hand, detected a reforming, "civilising" impulse from the very beginning, in such seemingly minor enactments as the ukase of January 3, 1683 curbing unruly behavior on the streets of Moscow,[5] the repeal of the death penalty for "seditious utterances",[6] and the substitution of the cutting off of ears instead of hands for certain categories of theft.[7] Later measures which Solov'ev considered praiseworthy included penalties against littering the streets of Moscow with "dung, carrion and all manner of vile excrement"[8] and the abolition of the practice of burying women alive for the murder of their husbands.[9]

Neither point of view is entirely satisfactory when considering the domestic achievements of Sophia's regency, which were for the most part inconsistent and piecemeal; but Solov'ev's positive assessment comes nearer to the truth in respect of foreign policy, which was both vigorously and consistently conducted. At the center of the busy diplomatic activity of the period stook Vasily Golitsyn, whose personal influence can be detected in all the major international business of those years.

As has already been mentioned, in the autumn of 1682 Golitsyn received the title of "Guardian of the state's great ambassadorial affairs", an honor which had been conferred on two of his predecessors in the foreign office, A.S. Matveev and A.L. Ordin-Nashchokin. In 1682 envoys were sent all over Europe -- Poland, Austria, Brandenburg, the Dutch Republic, England, Sweden and Denmark -- bearing charters of amity to foreign rulers from Sophia's regime.[10] This comprehensive operation was to set the pace of diplomatic activity during Golitsyn's term of office, when Russian was to make her presence felt in Europe as never before.

On entering the chancellery, Golitsyn found Russia's foreign affairs in a state of flux. There was no immediate threat of war, peace having been made with Turkey and the Crimea in 1681. The treaties of Andrusovo (1667) with Poland and Kardis (1661) with Sweden were still in operation, and although neither of these agreements was entirely satisfactory to Moscow, there were strong arguments for maintaining the status quo, especially in view of the regime's ostensibly "caretaker" role. But, as the next seven years were to prove, Russia's old defensive "fringe" role in European affairs was becoming more and more untenable. In May 1683 a treaty of mutual aid against Turkey was signed by King John of Poland and Emperor Leopold of Austria, who were joined in 1684 by the Venetian Republic. One of the points agreed upon by the allies was that they should attract other Christian monarchs to their cause, including the tsars of Muscovy. Golitsyn faced no easy task in evaluating the overtures of the numerous delegations which visited Moscow from 1683 onwards and also had to contend with differences of opinion at home. Hetman Ivan Samoilovich, for example, considered it foolhardy to abandon the hard-won peace with Turkey in return for the dubious advantages of friendship with the Poles, "a deceitful and unrealiable crowd, inveterate enemies of the Muscovite and Cossack peoples."[11] Religious differences, the interests of the sultan's Orthodox subjects, the dangers of Polish "treachery" all had to be weighed against the possibilities of either a separate Polish victory over the Turks and Tatars or a Turkish victory over the Poles with the subsequent likelihood of encroachment upon Muscovite territory. In 1682 the Poles had confirmed Samoilovich's misgivings by taking advantage of the turmoil in Moscow to stir up dissension in Left Bank Ukraine. The confirmation in office of Sophia's regime, however, ensured that future encounters would take place around the conference table. The first of several Polish delegations met a Russian contingent headed by Yakov Odoevsky and Ivan Buturlin at the border village of Andrusovo in early January 1684.[12] The Poles must have felt their hand strengthened by events of September the previous year when King John Sobieski had led allied armies to lift the Turkish siege of Vienna; but Golitsyn had briefed his delegates that "permanent peace" and a satisfactory settlement of the border question were prerequisite for Moscow's entry into any alliance. The Poles continued to insist that the territorial dispute could be settled only after Russia had agreed to an alliance. Both sides engaged in pro forma squabbles, the Russians accusing the Poles of violating the truce and misusing the tsar's titles, the Poles protesting at Russia's "harboring" of the renegade hetman Doroshenko and at her ban on the recruitment of cossacks in the war with Turkey.[13] The talks broke down in February, with nothing more than an agreement to ratify the truce.

The pressing situation in the south was to take precedence over any thought of territorial gain in the north. Early in 1683 the future Swedish resident in Moscow Christopher von Kochen arrived for talks and in June Russian envoys were sent for negotiations on the ratification of the Treaty of Kardis.[14]

Golitsyn's activities in the Foreign Office show him to have been not only a keen student of foreign affairs but also an enthusiastic cultivator of personal contacts with foreigners, a tendency which had already emerged in his dealings with Patrick Gordon. Shortly after Easter 1683 Golitsyn dined with the Dutch resident von Keller, one of the longest serving envoys in Moscow. Keller records that the minister arrived in one of four carriages bearing Russian dignitaries. "More than one glass of good wine was emptied by the gentlemen to the well-being of the state and the health of Their Majesties, and wishes were expressed for the best ties of friendship and understanding, which had prevailed for many years."[15] After dinner Golitsyn, always eager for first-hand knowledge, spoke with von Keller about Dutch military and financial affairs. Another foreigner who met Golitsyn in 1683 was the traveler, naturalist and student of Japan Engelbert Kämpfer, who came to Russia in June with a Swedish party en route for Persia. During an audience with the tsars Kämpfer took special note of "the chancellor Prince Wassili Golitzyn", who stood to the right of the tsars and conducted the reception on their behalf.[16] Kämpfer dined with the prince on at least one occasion, at which there were plentiful supplies of beer, brandy and new wine.[17]

1684 was a particularly busy year for Golitsyn, with delegations arriving from Poland, Sweden, Denmark and Austria and with individual travellers, domestic business and personal matters to deal with besides. On January 9 Tsar Ivan, now eighteen years old, was married to the young noblewoman Praskov'ia Fedorovna Saltykova.[18] Under different circumstances the tsar's mental and physical disabilities might have inclined his advisors to counsel celibacy, but Sophia had strong

33

political motives for marrying him off, both to signify his coming of age, traditionally marked by marriage, and to consolidate his claim to rule as "senior" tsar by continuing the Romanov dynasty through the Miloslav-sky line. Rumors must have been rife at the time, for even the Austrian envoy Johann Hövel, who visited Moscow only briefly at the beginning of February, was able to report that Ivan was being used as a "pawn" by the power-hungry Sophia, whose plans were to obtain heirs from him and his wife before Peter was old enough to marry.[19] We do not know whether Golitsyn attended the nuptials or took any direct part in Sophia's manipulations. More likely his thoughts were occupied by the negotiations then being conducted with Poland, as is confirmed by a conversation with Patrick Gordon on January 16. In a "secret conference" they discussed the situation in the Ukraine and the advisability of an alliance with Poland and Austria. Gordon seemed to favor a campaign against the Crimea, which was to be part of Russia's contribution to the proposed alliance, but was, like Samoilovich, uneasy about Polish intentions and other difficulties. Gordon was asked to produce a written report on the subject, which he did the next day.[20] He set out the possible objections to a campaign, but then countered them with a list of arguments in favor of an alliance. He dismissed any doubts about the success of a campaign in the Crimea, portraying Russia as heroically destroying the alien "nest" which had for so long harrassed and threatened Christendom.[21] As was noted earlier, talks with Poland broke down in February 1684, but not before Golitsyn had formulated Russia's conditions for an alliance, no doubt persuaded by many of Gordon's arguments. At the beginning of May Gordon left for Kiev and was asked to write to Golitsyn about the situation there.[22]

Golitsyn's attention was next turned to Swedish affairs, although steps now being taken towards an alliance with Poland and the concentration of forces in the south meant that these were of secondary importance. Preparations for the arrival of the Swedish delegation in Moscow were nonetheless elaborate. On February 17 Muscovite servitors resident within 250 versts of the capital were ordered to assemble for the reception of the visitors, on pain of relegation to the ranks and partial confiscation of estates.[23] In April assorted tables, mattresses and other items were requisitioned through the Foreign Office for delegates' use, and orders were given for the cleaning and redecoration of the premises they were to occupy, for the replacement of window panes and the construction of extensions and pavements.[24] April 28 saw the arrival of the ambassadors, headed by Conrad Gyldenstierne, Jonas Kling-

Golitsyn's House

stedt and Otto Stakeberg.[25] In the talks which followed, conducted for the Russian side by Golitsyn in person, the Russians tried to obtain concessions by referring to Swedish breaches of etiquette. In 1669, for example, it was claimed that the King of Sweden had used the title grand prince instead of tsar in a letter to the King of Poland. He had enquired about the tsar's health not personally but through a secretary. Reports of the Stenka Razin rebellion (1670-71) issued in Sweden had "dishonored" the Russian crown. In 1676 the Governor-General of Riga had referred to Tsar Fedor by the patronymic Mikhailovich, and so on.[26] Golitsyn, it seems, had not abandoned the Muscovite negotiating technique of his era, which entailed petty point-scoring and quibbling over protocol in an attempt to wear down the opposition. In compensation for Sweden's "lapses" over the years he demanded the return of "Russian" towns on the Baltic. These claims were not pressed, and may have been introduced as a matter of form in order that Moscow's traditional pretensions to territory under Swedish rule should not appear to have lapsed. In a second meeting on May 10 the Swedes showed themselves to be adept at the same game. The Russians, they claimed, had called their king Carlus instead of Carolus. They demanded the renewal of border markers, the establishment of permanent ambassadors or "residents" in Moscow and Stockholm and the reduction of taxes for Swedes living in Russia.[27] On May 22 disputes were settled and a treaty was drawn up which, whilst maintaining the status quo on the border question, included assurances over the use of royal titles, on religious toleration, provisions for envoys and free trade.[28] On May 28 the document was signed by both tsars in a ceremony at which Golitsyn officiated, welcoming the envoys and handing the ratified charter to them.[29] The following day Sophia greeted the Swedes in an additonal ceremony also attended by Golitsyn.[30] One of the main clauses of the treaty concerned free trade between the two countries, which already had close commercial ties. The Swedes were allowed to maintain warehouses and stalls in a number of towns.[31]

Some criticism has been leveled at Golitsyn for the somewhat neutral outcome of the talks with Sweden. Tereshchenko, for example, argued that he should have taken advantage of Sweden's current weakness by pressing for a renegotiation of the treaty and extra territory for Muscovy. He was "bought out by the Swedes not only in this but also in other matters."[32] In view of the turn of events in the south, however, Russia required above all the neutralisation of Sweden, and from this point of view the talks of 1683-84 were by no means fruitless.

Golitsyn was not allowed to forget the Ukrainian question. Two weeks after the arrival of the Swedes an Austrian delegation came to Moscow, with whom talks were conducted more or less simultaneously. Austrian overtures had begun with the visit at the beginning of February of Johann Hövel, sent by the emperor to propose an alliance against the Turks.[33] (In an interesting aside on his visit he reports that Tsar Ivan, who received him on February 8, seemed on the verge of collapse and had to be supported by two attendants.) The Austrian legation that arrived on May 14, 1684 was more high-powered, being headed by Johann Christian Zierowski and Sebastian von Blumberg.[34] In the presence of the tsars, Blumberg invited Muscovy to join the military alliance against the Turks, but it was not until the middle of June that Golitsyn stated his terms: "If the Polish king cedes the city of Kiev to Their Majesties the Tsars, Their Majesties the Tsars will, in alliance with the king, wage war against the Crimean khan."[35] Blumberg assured him that "the Red Sea with impatience waits to embrace you... All Greece and Asia await you."

The delegates left Moscow at the end of June, having also made progress in promoting the rights of Catholics to practise their faith in Russia. Golitsyn had already expressed some sympathy for Catholic grievances when on January 31 he had been approached by Patrick Gordon, one of the spokesmen for Moscow's tiny Catholic community, and reminded that Catholics did not enjoy the same privileges as Protestants in the practice of their religion. The prince had advised him to apply to the tsars, with a hint that concessions would probably be forthcoming.[36] On June 14 Imperial Secretary Maurizio Vota arrived for talks on the Catholic question. He was favorably impressed by the foreign minister, describing a meeting on June 19 when he "was taken to the residence of Prince Golitsyn, the prime minister and worthy to rule a kingdom." The prince received him "with distinction", and after various entertainments he promised to arrange an audience with the tsars, an honor for which Vota was apparently unprepared.[37] The concession eventually obtained allowed two Jesuits to reside in Moscow under the protection of the Viennese court, the first to arrive being a German priest, Father Schmidt.[38] A temporary chapel was offered by a Dutch merchant on his own premises.

The last of the major talks of 1684 were conducted with the Danes. A treaty signed on August 10 laid down various points of diplomatic protocol, for example envoys were to attend audiences without hats or swords, and stipulated subsistence payments to envoys. The allowances seemed generous in the extreme; each ambassador, for example, was to be allowed a daily drink allotment of eight cups of fortified wine, one measure of Spanish wine, one measure of Rhine wine, one of currant, raspberry and blackcurrant cordial, one of mead, ¾ of sweet mead, one bucket of "good" mead and two buckets of beer.[39]

The most detailed first-hand portrait of Golitsyn to survive from 1684 was written by Dr. Laurent Rinhuber, who came to Moscow in June with a letter from the Elector of Saxony, one of the allies in the battle of Vienna in 1683. As one of Rinhuber's biographers remarked, the doctor was "playing" at being a diplomat, his real reasons for coming to Russia being both "touristic" and personal.[40] In December 1683 he had received a letter from the Dutch resident von Keller urging him "on no account to miss the opportunity of speaking with Prince Vasily Vasil'evich Golitsyn, the first minister of state."[41] The doctor followed this advice and was kindly received by Golitsyn, who seemed "very graciously disposed" towards him.[42] On June 20 Golitsyn arranged an audience with the tsars, at which he personnaly accepted letters from the Elector and Duke Frederick of Saxony and handed them to the sovereigns.[43] Rinhuber provides a rare glimpse of the prince's private life and further ratification of his receptive attitude towards foreigners and curiosity about their countries and customs. On June 22 the doctor accepted an invitation to visit Golitsyn on his country estate at Chernaia Griaz' to the south of Moscow, where he was received by the prince in person. He presented Golitsyn with two gold medallions bearing the Elector's portrait and coat of arms. Golitsyn was obviously pleased by the gift and Rinhuber was asked whether he had a portrait of the Elector for the perusal of the tsars and had to promise to bring one on his next visit. Golitsyn plied the doctor with questions, some of which showed a certain naivety on the Russian's part, as well as eagerness to obtain the snippets of foreign news that still penetrated infrequently into Russia. He asked how many Electors there were, whether they were really responsible for choosing the emperor and why they were not all assisting him against Turkey. He inquired about the political situation in Saxony and questioned Rinhuber about his own movements since receiving the Elector's letters which were now over a year old. Had the doctor visited Holland and England? Was the plague still raging? Had he been in "unclean places"? He also mentioned Rinhuber's desire to go to Persia, offering him safe conduct and transport, but Rinhuber was obliged to explain that he wished to return to Germany before undertaking the journey.[44]

Rinhuber seemed in no hurry to return. He was still in Moscow in mid-July, when Golitsyn suffered a serious fall whilst inspecting some building work in the Kremlin palace. He injured his head and sprained his shoulders. After lying in a fever for some time, bound in linen cloths, he summoned Rinhuber, who prescribed various remedies, including the application of an enema.[45] Golitsyn recovered in about two weeks and was so grateful that Rinhuber was frequently invited to his table and on some occasions spent the night in an antechamber of Golitsyn's house. Despite these auspicious developments, however, Rinhuber was not shieled from the vagaries of Muscovite diplomatic protocol. On August 18 he was called to the Foreign Office and rebuked for miswriting the tsars' titles in a letter. He was warned that "if the Lord Golitsyn were not your patron you would, by the tsars' law, be exiled to Siberia."[46] The miswording was nothing more serious than the use of "Ivan and Peter Alekseevich" instead of the approved "Ivan Alekseevich and Peter Alekseevich",[47] but he was ordered to rewrite the offending document. Rinhuber was in no doubt that he got off lightly thanks to Golitsyn's influence, even though the prince did not overrule his subordinates. "Although the Lord Golitsyn was by nature clement and humane, still he was obliged by reason of his office and out of respect for his colleagues... to make himself out to be strict and command that I sign the slightly corrected aforementioned clause."[48]

On August 27 Rinhuber again rode out to Chernaia Griaz', where he witnessed the consecration of a wooden church recently constructed on the estate. Tsar Ivan and his wife and Sophia also attended the ceremony. Watching from the sidelines, Rinhuber saw the arrival of their carriages from nearby Kolomenskoe.[49] After the two-hour service, Golitsyn provided refreshments of locally grown apples and brandy. Rinhuber was invited to accompany the party back to the manor hourse, which he found to be "graced by nature with green meadows, brooks, springs, shrubbery and hills and a beautiful prospect."[50] In the house the doctor met Golitsyn's wife, a rare sighting of this retiring lady, who offered each guest a goblet of brandy in welcome. Thirty people sat down to dinner. Rinhuber was placed at the prince's side and was highly honored to be told: "Doctor, you must stay in our country, for you speak and write our language and have also served the tsars before this." Golitsyn's high regard for foreign personnel had been expressed on a number of occasions, but luckily for Rinhuber, who had no desire to re-enter Muscovite service, the invitation was not pressed. After the meal the guests were entertained by musicians who performed songs "in the Greek manner."[51] On Russian New Year's Day, September 1, Rinhuber had his last meeting with Golitsyn and departed shortly afterwards.

In addition to the major and minor diplomatic business already recorded, Golitsyn had many other matters to deal with in 1684. He was in constant communication with Hetman Samoilovich, whose views on the Ukrainian/Turkish situation did not always coincide with his own. If relations between the two were strained, however, there was no hint of it in a letter dated February 24, in which the hetman addressed the prince as "my most gracious friend and benefactor", adding his full titles and informing him that the Poles had been encroaching on Russian territory. He asked Golitsyn to persuade the tsars to intervene with the Polish authorities and, as a parting gesture of goodwill, informed the prince that he was sending him a barrel of wine, which he advised him to store in his cellar for at least four weeks in order to obtain the optimum color and taste.[52] Later in the year, despite his intransigence on the Polish question, Samoilovich made himself useful to the government in Moscow by preparing for the election of a new Metropolitan of Kiev, who was to be subordinated to the Patriarch of Moscow. There were political motives behind this move, for it was deemed necessary to remove Ukrainian religious affairs from the influence of the Uniates on Polish territory and from the jurisdiction of the Patriarch of Constantinople, who lived under Turkish rule. The new metropolitan, Gedeon, was appointed in July 1685, to the satisfaction of both Moscow and Samoilovich, who was able to settle some personal scores with local clergymen.[53] Golitsyn's work in the Foreign Office involved him in a wide variety of activities, even though the inclusion of his name in documents of the period was sometimes a mere formality and much of the work was carried out by assistants. In January 1684, for example, he received a memorandum from the Musketeer Chancellery about one Matvei Sidorov, who had been arrested for unruly behavior, smoking, taking snuff, shouting and drinking in the early hours of the morning.[54] In April the Foreign Office dealt with the application of the enterprising Dutch merchant Elias Tabert to set up textile mills near Moscow. After a thorough investigation of Tabert's record, Golitsyn authorised the issue of a licence allowing him a ten-year period of duty-free manufacture and trade with the provision that he employ Russian apprentices.[55] In November 1682 a similar operation, that of Abraham Paulus or Paulson from Hamburg, had been approved. He and his business were placed under the jurisdiction of the Foreign Office in November 1684 and provided a useful service by supplying costly cloths such as velvets, silks and satins for the royal wardrobe and for gifts to ambassadors and servitors.[56] In May-June the office was entrusted with delivering 20 "German" horses from Lübeck,[57] dealt with the casting of a large bell in Chernigov,[58] with lists of birds of prey in the royal hawkery[59] and the interminable disturbances among the Don Cossacks.[60] It had to issue a reprimand to post drivers who had been causing delays in the postal service to Riga[61] and to deal with complaints from foreign merchants in Archangel about ill-treatment by the local governor.[62] On July 23 the chancellery sent instructions to the St. Savva Monastery in Zvenigorod (one of the large monasteries under its jurisdiction) for the preparation of quantities of beer, ale, kvas, sour cabbage and mead for the tsars' forthcoming visit.[63] In November Golitsyn was ordered to put a stop to the illicit trade in tobacco by Tatars on Foreign Office premises.[64]

In addition there were matters of a more directly diplomatic nature, including the maintenance of correspondence with foreign courts and dignitaries. In November, for example, Golitsyn wrote to Prince Oginski, the new chancellor of Lithuania, congratulating him on his appointment and apologising for his failure to reply to a letter, explaining that "this happened only because of my engagement in the sovereigns' current affairs and other such matters and also because the postal service was subject to delays."[65] That same erratic postal service brought the foreign dispatches, transcribed for the most part from the German Kuranten and which it would have been one of Golitsyn's tasks to read. April-December 1684 brought reports about events in Rome, the Ukraine, Hungary, Austria, Poland, the Baltic states and Holland, a range of news on wars, treaties and diplomatic developments which made the employees of the Foreign Office potentially the best informed men in Muscovy.[66]

These varied duties did not exhaust the responsibilities of Golitsyn and his chancellery. The prikaz also had its own artistic and architectural workshops and work carried out in 1684 included the renovation of the Kremlin Palace of Facets[67] and repairs and renovations to the foreign office premises, including the painting of a fresco depicting the heavenly bodies with clouds (svetila nebesnyia s oblaki) in one of the upper chambers, an example of the secular currents which penetrated Russian art in the 1680s.[68] As will be shown later, Golitsyn was himself an active patron of architecture and connoisseur of art. A number of Tsarevna Sophia's architectural projects were also carried out by foreign office builders and craftsmen.

In view of the successes, honors and responsibilities which Golitsyn's career had already brought him, it comes as something of a surprise to find that early in 1684 he submitted a petition couched in the most humble of terms in which he described his service record for the years 1676 to 1682 and reminded the sovereigns that "in the course of the aforementioned services namely the Chigirin campaigns and others at that time, and as a result of the damage from the conflagration [i.e. the fire in his home in 1680] I incurred many debts and was obliged to sell a village of 60 households. And I, your slave, have only 320 peasant households held in service and hereditary tenure in various towns."[69] Golitsyn's plea was not in itself unusual, for unpaid or underpaid allowances and salaries were a common bone of contention for seventeenth-century Russian servitors. The government responded favorably. An examination of Golitsyn's service record was made and on March 23, 1684 a charter was issued addressed to Golitsyn and to all officers who had served in the campaigns of 1676-80. The prince was awarded a sable-lined robe, a gilded silver cup, a 200-ruble supplement to his salary and five of his service estates, villages in Suzdal', Riazan', Yaroslavl', Kozel'sk and Odoev, were converted to hereditary tenure.[70] The robe, which was specially made in the royal treasury in April, was embroided with plant motifs on a silver background. The fur, obtained from the Siberian Chancellery, and the satin were valued at the considerable sum of 393 rubles, 5 altyn.[71]

It is possible that Golitsyn was persuaded to submit the petition in order to consolidate his credentials and bring his earlier career to public notice, but by the end of 1684 he had established himself firmly in his new post and was building a reputation both in Russian and abroad.

1685 proved to be a quieter year, punctuated by the arrival of Austrian and Polish envoys in continuing attempts to conclude an alliance. In April Johann Kurz arrived from Vienna,[72] and in August the Pole Zembocki came for a conference on the border dispute.[73] The year also saw the outbreak of a territorial conflict which must have seemed remote in comparison to events in the West. In July Chinese troops attacked the Russian fortified settlement of Albazin on the Amur River in a culmination of antagonisms which had been simmering ever since Russian pioneers first penetrated the region in the 1630s-40s. The war that followed was finally brought to an end by the Treaty of Nerchinsk, negotiated by ambassador Fedor Golovin in the summer of 1689.[74] The intricately worded settlement, which ceded much of the Amur region to China but left part of the border undefined, was of considerable significance for the future of Sino-Russian relations, but seems to have had comparatively little bearing on Golitsyn's career, the signing coming too late (August 27, 1689) to contribute to the downfall of Sophia's already tottering regime. Golitsyn's interest in Eastern affairs appears to have been subordinated to his involvement in the West, especially when one considers that the main negotiations with the Chinese were in progress at a time when the prince was occupied with the Crimean campaigns.

At the end of April Golitsyn retired to his estate at Chernaia Griaz' for a brief rest, but was not spared the steady stream of dispatches from Moscow.[75] Amongst the many matters which passed through his hands during the year were a request from the King of Sweden for the construction of new merchants' warehouses in Moscow[76] and an appeal from some musketeers in Pskov seeking permission to enter a monastery without paying the customary entrance fee.[77] In August a batch of gifts arrived from the Queen of Georgia, including a set of silver candalabra and some pillow cases. These were delivered to the royal family by Golitsyn in person.[78] The Don region continued to be a source of anxiety. There were regular reports about the activities of Old Believers, who were "enticing" Cossacks to join them. In October Golitsyn received a delegation from the Don reporting on one such case.[79]

At the beginning of 1686 Golitsyn dined with Patrick Gordon and fellow Scot Paul Menezies, who again mentioned the problems of Catholics in the Foreign Colony.[80] On January 28 Gordon, who after much petitioning had finally obtained permission to visit Britain, came to Chernaia Griaz' to take his leave of the prince.[81] Golitsyn asked him to write "by every post." Later in the year, in Edinburgh, Gordon was to receive a letter from Golitsyn asking him to hire officers "of inferiour quality" and "some engeniers, fireworkers and minirers, and to promise them yearly pay, according to their quality, and liberty to go out of the country when their occasions required."[82] The assurances on the right of exit may have been added for the benefit of the intermediary, for Gordon had good cause to warn prospective emigrants of the difficulties of escaping from Muscovite service. During this trip Gordon's wife and children were held in Russia as hostages to ensure his return. In attempting to hire foreigners Golitsyn was, of course, breaking no new ground. The policy had been employed by both Ivan III and Ivan IV in the 15th-16th centuries, and had reached a significant scale by the reign of Tsar Aleksei, who in 1652 had established the separate Foreign Colony

(<u>nemetskaia sloboda</u>) for the accommodation of foreigners in Moscow.

Meanwhile resolution of the Polish dilemma was
approaching. For many Cossacks "alliance" with Poland
was already a <u>fait accompli</u>. Reports arrived in 1684-85
from the prince's informants in the Ukraine and Poland
that thousands of Zaporozhian Cossacks, subjects of the
tsars, were joining up to fight against the Turks.[83]
Protests to the Polish government met with the response
that the Cossacks were acting out of "Christian love
and zeal, for the sake of the Christian peoples... and
their (actions) were deserving not of reproach but of
praise."[84] Golitsyn must have been anxious lest the
Cossacks' already shaky loyalty to Moscow should be
further undermined by the government's failure to oppose the Turks and Tatars. In addition, Moscow was now
in a better position to obtain concessions from the
Poles in return for military aid, for since the heroic
siege of Vienna the war had gone badly for Poland, with
Hetman Stanislaw Jablonowski being forced to withdraw
from Moldavia with heavy losses in 1685. Nor, in spite
of Samoilovich's warning about exchanging "golden peace
for iron war", was the prospect of settling old scores
with the Tatars entirely uncongenial. The Tatars continued to exact tribute payments and to mistreat Russian
envoys. The Turkish sultan had not agreed to all the
clauses of the Treaty of Bakhchisarai until 1685, and
even then many had been violated.[85] Even so opinion in
Moscow was divided. Sophia and Golitsyn were now inclined towards an alliance, but a dissident faction at
court, headed by Prince P.I. Prozorovsky and F.P. Sal-
tykov continued to oppose the idea.[86]

At the beginning of February 1686 a Polish delegation headed by plenipotentiary ambassadors Krzysztof
Grzymultowski, the Governor of Poznan, and Chancellor
Marcjan Oginski of Lithuania arrived in Moscow.[87] Both
sides were determined to impress. The Polish contingent
numbered about a thousand and was treated to a show of
Muscovite ceremonial and military strength. On their
way to a grand reception in the palace the Poles stopped outside Golitsyn's mansion to inspect the guard,
who saluted them with a trumpet fanfare.[88] The negotia-
tors met ten times, with Golitsyn acting on behalf of
the tsars. The talks contained the familiar mixture of
the serious and the trivial, the Russians trying to
score points by complaining, for example, that the
Poles had placed seals upside down on rescripts to the
tsars and had misused titles (Ivan instead of Ioann,
Mikhail Mikhailovich instead of Aleksei Mihailovich and
so on).[89] No agreement could be reached on the crucial
issue of Kiev and the amount of indemnity to be paid
for its permanent cession to Moscow. On March 27 the

43

Polish delegation prepared to leave, but then came up with fresh concessions, expressing their willingness to give up Kiev in return for towns on the lower Dniepr. Haggling continued until the middle of April when the Poles again threatened to leave, but on April 26 a treaty, partially drafted by Golitsyn himself, was signed. Its 33 articles included the establishment of "permanent peace" between the signatories, the cession of Kiev and its immediate hinterland to Moscow and the ratification of Muscovite control of Smolensk, Roslavl', Dorogobuzh and Zaporozh'e. In return Russia was to sever relations with Turkey and the Crimea, undertake military operations against the Tatars and pay Poland compensation of 146,000 rubles. In addition the treaty contained clauses on the royal titles, religious toleration and trade.[90] On April 27 the Polish ambassadors had a private audience with the tsars, with Golitsyn in attendance. Toasts were proposed and after the tsars had retired Sophia came in to congratulate the delegations.[91]

The Treaty of Moscow signalled Moscow's most notable entry to date into European affairs. One of the clauses stipulated that the signatories should seek the aid of other Christian monarchs and a number of Muscovite delegations were sent to Europe for this purpose, although without achieving any positive results. The missions of Prince Ya.F. Dolgoruky and I.E. Myshetsky to France and Spain in 1687 resulted in an embarrassing diplomatic incident with the French and nothing but vague assurances of friendship from the Spaniards. It has been suggested that approaches to both these countries were inappropriate and underlined Moscow's continuing ignorance of the nuances of the political situation in the West.[92] Other missions included those of V.T. Posnikov to Prussia, Holland, England and Florence, B. Mikhailov to Denmark and B.P. Sheremet'ev and I.I. Chaadaev to Austria.[93] The King of Denmark agreed to make his fleet available in case of "dire necessity", but there were no other significant responses.[94]

Sophia regarded the treaty as a personal triumph, both for herself and Golitsyn. The acquisition of Kiev, the "mother of Russian cities", had special patriotic connotations, and Polish concessions over the royal titles were also prized.[95] From now on Sophia began with increasing frequency to place herself on a par with her brothers in public ceremonies and in the wording of rescripts and decrees. A continuation of the "New Chronicle", the official record of Russian history, was compiled in the Foreign Office, bringing events up to 1686 and ending with the Treaty of Moscow.[96]

Golitsyn was richly rewarded. On June 29 a laudatory proclamation were read out in the presence of the royal family "By the decree of the great sovereigns, tsars and grand princes Ivan Alekseevich and Peter Alekseevich and the great sovereign lady, the noble tsarevna and grand princes Sophia Alekseevna, autocrats of all the Great and Little and White Russias, the sovereigns' favor is expressed to their privy councillor and guardian Prince Vasily Vasil'evich Golitsyn in the great sovereigns' presence."98 The value of Golitsyn's reward for successfully negotiating the treaty was computed by reference to honors conferred upon his predecessors for similar services to the crown. It was discovered, for example, that A.L. Ordin-Nashchokin had received a silver cup, a sable-lined robe and 400 rubles for the Treaty of Andrusovo in 1667.98 Golitsyn subsequently received a gold cup weighing $2\frac{1}{2}$ puds, a sable-lined satin robe worth 400 rubles, a 250-ruble supplement to his salary and hereditary tenure of 3,000 peasant households in the Nizhny Novgorod region, "with large and small villages, peasants, laborers, arable lands and all productive resources."99

One of the by-products of Russia's treaty with Poland was the granting of further concessions to Catholics in Moscow, a matter which Patrick Gordon had again mentioned to Golitsyn before his departure for Scotland at the beginning of the year.100 At the time Golitsyn had advised him to be patient. The Treaty of Moscow now guaranteed immunity from persecution and forced conversion, but remained silent on the issue of permission for a public chapel; the relevant clause simply stated that foreign Catholics in Moscow were to be "free to practise their faith in their homes."101 On June 4 Emperor Leopold of Austria wrote a letter requesting the right of public worship.102 It was delivered by the Jesuit Georgius David, who came in the capacity of second priest to the Moscow community under the provisions of 1684. David arrived in the capital in August 1686 and soon received cordial greetings from Golitsyn, who sent an interpreter to inquire about his journey.103 The Jesuit became a great admirer of Golitsyn, but not even the prince's considerable influence and favorable attitude towards Catholics were able to break through the patriarch's abhorrence of foreign prayer houses. No permanent Catholic chapel was erected during Sophia's regency.104

In the latter half of 1686 Golitsyn was again required to deal with the problem of schismatics on territory administered by the Foreign Office. Religious disturbances in the capital has subsided after Sophia's confrontation with the Old Believers in 1682, but the problem of "underground" dissenters in remote hermitages and retreats continued unabated. In November 1682 rescripts had been sent to Church prelates all over the

45

country, urging them to bring dissenters to trial, and in April 1685 a long decree reiterated the penalties laid down for religious dissent in Tsar Aleksei's reign, e.g. the death sentence for "detractors of the faith" who failed to go to confession, had their children accepted into the Old Belief or persuaded others to commit suicide by burning.[105] Despite the harsh penalties, throughout 1685-86 Golitsyn received reports of incidents in the south. In May 1686, for example, the Governor of Voronezh sent news of a dissident encampment on the River Medveditsa and in response the Don Cossack ataman Frol Minaev was instructed to root out and destroy all such settlements.[106] In June a group of Orthodox priests and Cossack representatives came to the foreign office with first-hand reports on dissident colonies and handed over confiscated service books.[107]

On September 1 Golitsyn greeted Gordon, newly returned from abroad. He was eager for all the latest news and invited the Scot to dinner on September 3 and again on the 10th, the latter occasion at Chernaia Griaz'. As Gordon reported, "after dinner, had much discourse, yet nothing of carrying on the warr, only of my jorney and my effaires. Wee went to hunting afterwards, and I tooke my leave in the field."[108] Gordon must have been disappointed not to obtain more information about the alliance with Poland, especially as he had been absent during the negotiations. Shortly afterwards Gordon and the prince fell out in an incident that reflects somewhat badly on the latter. On November 5 Gordon "spoke to the Boyar about sending for my wyfe, who gave me a dubious answer."[109] On November 22 "the Boyar did fall out in a great passion againt me." He ordered Gordon's demotion to the rank of ensign, evidently in annoyance at the Scot's persistent pleas about being reunited with his wife and, more serious, his efforts to terminate his service in Russia. On September 15 the Dutch resident Von Keller had handed the tsars a letter from the King of England requesting his release from service and matters were further complicated by the "honoring" of Gordon with the post of Envoy Extraordinary to the tsars.[110] Gordon continues: "The Boyar also, with very high words, and threats, and reasoning, without all reason, or the least show of uprightness, or valuing, or considering anything I said, insisted still that I should acknowledge my error, and crave pardon and promise to serve in the future."[111] Gordon was obliged to eat humble pie and submit a written apology, but his disgrace was short-lived and good relations between the two men were quickly restored. Golitsyn's irritable reaction at the prospect of losing one of his most experienced foreign

officers, either abroad or to another post, was directly connected with the recent announcement of Russia's
forthcoming campaign against the Tatars. The prince's
own duties as diplomat and statesman were soon to be
exchanged, probably unwillingly, for those of military
commander.

# CHAPTER FOUR

## THE CRIMEAN CAMPAIGNS

The forthcoming campaign against the Tatars was announced on September 3, 1686.[1] State servitors were ordered to join the colors and in November a tax was levied to fund the war. It was announced that the campaign was to be undertaken to rid Russia of unendurable humiliations and abuses, including the persecutions of Christians, violation of her territory, the dishonoring of envoys and the exactions of tribute imposed by the "infidels".[2] Little stress was laid upon the wider international implications of the war. Golitsyn now added the title "household commander of the great regiment" to his others. He was to be commander-in-chief of the whole army and to be aided by four generals: A.S. Shein, V.D. Dolgoruky, M.G. Romodanovsky and I.Yu. Leont'ev.[3]

It has been suggested that Golitsyn was far from overjoyed by the new appointment. De la Neuville writes: "Prince Golitsyn proposed several nobles capable of this task, but it was told him by common consent that since he had made the peace with Poland, he himself must take the trouble to see whether the conquest of Perekop was as easy as he claimed. He did everything possible to refuse the post, adjudging rightly, clever man that he was, that he might encounter great difficulties for which he would be held responsible; and that in spite of all the precautions and provisions he might make, it would be hard to save his reputation if he failed, as, even though he was given an army formidable in respect of numbers, they were nothing but a multitude of peasants, poor soldiers little inured to war, with which he would never be able to carry out vigorous operations and emerge with honor, being more great a politician and man of the cabinet than a great general. He was well aware that the risks involved in his absence from Moscow outweighed the dubious possibility of victories and that his enemies were eager for him to take command of the armies in order to diminish his authority at home."[4]

De la Neuville, writing some time after the notorious failure of both Crimean campaigns, may well have overestimated Golitsyn's fears. In 1686 failure was by no means certain, neither was Golitsyn himself totally inexperienced in military matters. Fears about the undermining of his influence in Moscow while he was away in the south were probably more genuine, and were subsequently expressed in a series of letters to Fedor Shaklovity, written during the campaigns, in which he

requested news of all formal gatherings and receptions
in Moscow and tried to gauge public reaction to his
activities, as, for example, on the occasion when he
publically drank to the health of Sophia alongside the
customary toasts to the tsars at the beginning of the
campaign.[5] He was anxious about potential enemies in
Moscow, such as Prince M.A. Cherkassky, a leading courtier and soldier. "Keep an ever watchful eye on Ch.,"
he pleaded, "and take care that he does not succeed to
that position [as Peter's attendant] even if you have
to enlist the aid of the patriarch and elder tsarevnas
to prevent it."[6] The patriarch too, gave cause for concern. Apparently Joachim had objected to some vestments
which Golitsyn had donated to a church.[7] The slightest
delay in the arrival of Shaklovity's letters aroused
anxiety: "I beg you to write about what is going on
there and whether there is any treachery from those
troublemakers. You write nothing to me. I fear that you
have some grudge against me, but I have done you no
wrong."[8] He reacted with alarm to news of Shaklovity's
plans to visit him. "You should not come yourself. God
only knows what those scoundrels will get up to in your
absence."[9] His letters show that despite the success of
his years in office, Golitsyn was still unsure of his
ground and unduly sensitive about adverse comment and
criticism.

Whatever Golitsyn's fears may have been at the
beginning of 1687, Sophia seems to have been at the
height of her confidence. On January 8 a rescript was
issued reviewing the formulae for royal titles in charters of privilege (zhalovannye gramoty) since the reign
of Tsar Mikhail, and stipulating the following wording:
"By the decree of the great sovereigns, tsars and grand
princes Ioann Alekseevich and Peter Alekseevich and the
great sovereign lady, the noble tsarevna and grand
princess Sophia Alekseevna autocrats of all the Great
and Little and White Russias."[10] One may note the
shift, already observed in earlier documents, of
Sophia's titles to precede the word "autocrats", thus
establishing her as the third side of a ruling tri-
angle.

For Golitsyn the beginning of 1687 was not without
its lighter moments. On January 13 he and his son Aleksei attended the wedding of the daughter of Daniel
Hartmann, one of the leading merchants of the foreign
colony,[11] and on January 23 the new church dedicated to
St. Paraskeva Piatnitsa which Golitsyn had had built
next to his Moscow mansion was consecrated by the
patriarch.[12] But the forthcoming campaign was the major
concern. On February 2 Gordon drilled his brigade before Golitsyn and the royal family in the Kremlin and
was later congratulated by the prince for an impressive

display.[13] On February 17 Golitsyn departed for the Trinity-St. Sergius Monastery, having instructed Gordon to have his troops ready for his return on the 20th.[14] On February 22 icons and consecrated banners, to be carried to the war, were handed over to Golitsyn and his fellow officers in a religious ceremony, with the patriarch officiating and the tsars and Sophia in attendance. Prayers were read for victory over the Tatars and the commanding officers were blessed. Then Golitsyn, accompanied by the superior of the Kremlin Chudov Monastery, went to his mansion to witness the carrying of the banners, icons and crosses into the newly consecrated church. After the ceremony the prince invited members of the clergy into his home and treated them to vodka.[15]

Soon after this Golitsyn left for the south.[16] On May 2 he crossed the River Merl, not far from the Ukrainian town of Kolomak and on the 3rd he dined with Gordon and other foreign officers.[17] From the outset he was plagued with problems not the least being the slow mobilisation of troops and constant disputes amongst servitors over their assignment to units and ranks. In dispatches to Shaklovity Golitsyn reported that two junior officers, Prince B.F. Dolgoruky and Prince Yu.F. Shcherbatov, appeared on parade with their troops and horses all clad in black, evidently as a protest against the campaign and a prediction of its outcome, as well as an expression of discontent about their commissions and the use of new military formations.[18] Golitsyn appealed to the authorities in Moscow to devise a fitting punishment for the offenders and to send strongly worded reprimands, but later he relented and accepted their apologies. On May 30, 50,000 Cossacks under the command of Hetman Samoilovich joined the Russians on the River Samara, producing a combined force that has been variously estimated at between 100 - 200,000 men.[19] In addition to the main force, simultaneous operations were carried out by Don Cossacks in the east and a unit of Zaporozhians was sent down the Dniepr towards Kazikermen. The armies set off for the Crimea and reached the watering place of Konskie Vody in mid-June.

It was here that an unexpected hazard was encountered. Steppe fires, apparently started by Tatars in the vicinity, flared up and impeded the armies' progress. Writes Gordon: "On the 17th we were in a dreadful predicament, for it cost much pain and exertion to procure the requisite amount of grass to keep the horses alive, and it was reckoned that if the Tartars were to attack it would be impossible to obtain even this amount; the horses were already dropping and would be in no fit state to pull the cannons, not to mention the provision waggons."[20] There were reports that further on everything was scorched and burnt. According to the Swiss soldier Franz Lefort: "Our Generallissimus was beside himself and, I can assure you, wept most bitterly."[21] Golitsyn's own account of what happened is contained in a dispatch to the court, in which he claimed that after they had reached Konskie Vody and crossed the River Yanchokrak the khan was so perturbed at the size of the Russian armies that he took fright and refused to come out into the open. The Tatars remained in their villages but set fire to the steppe to impede the enemy. The Russians proceeded for several days although greatly inconvenienced by the heat, dust and flames and lack of water and fodder, until they came within 90 versts of Perekop. But when the enemy failed to appear and fodder shortages became critical, they decided to retreat, sending on the officer Nepluiev with a unit to engage the Tatars.[22]

There seems to be some discrepancy about the distance covered by the troops beyond Konskie Vody. According to Gordon on June 14 they progressed only two miles, reaching the Yanchokrak on the 15th and the Karachakrak on the 16th, at which point they were still 200 versts from the Crimea.[23] The decision to turn back was made on the 17th and by June 20 they arrived back at Konskie Vody.[24]

In his dispatches Golitsyn blamed the Tatars for the steppe fires, but soon rumours began to spread that the Cossacks were the culprits. Samoilovich, it will be recalled, had never been in favor of the campaign and it was even suggested that the subjugation of the Tatars was against the interest of the Cossacks, who would thus be deprived of their strategic significance and hence of their bargaining power with the Muscovite government. Whatever the truth of the rumors of Cossack sabotage, it must have been expedient to find a scapegoat and even De la Neuville, generally an admirer of Golitsyn, believed that "in order to exculpate himself at court for the campaign's lack of success, the prince did his best to shift the blame for his shortcomings onto Hetman Ivan Samoilovich."[25] If this is true, it reflects badly upon Golitsyn. There are hints that he may have been settling old personal scores with the hetman, who in 1677, for example, had sided with Romodanovsky in a dispute with the prince.[26] The blame-shifting exercise, if such it was, was expedient in more ways than one. Samoilovich, as it turned out, was unpopular in the Ukraine. In 1684 he had successfully defended himself against a charge of embezzling proceeds from the liquor franchise,[27] but equally serious charges were now presented not by Golitsyn but by a group of the hetman's own officers, who came to the prince to denounce Samoilovich and beg for his dismissal. In their complaint, lodged at the beginning of July, they referred to his ill-treatment of Cossacks, his arrogance, neglect of church-going and, more seriously, treasonable activities against the Muscovite government.[28] On July 12 Shaklovity arrived from Moscow with rescripts of praise and thanks to the troops and instructions, nearly all impracticable, for the continuation of the campaign.[29] No doubt he listened with interest to the charges against Samoilovich and at a council of war on July 14 it was decided to impeach the hetman. The proceedings that followed showed Golitsyn in a creditable light. He did not hesitate to question the motives of the Cossack officers in denouncing their leader and sent to Moscow for advice about what action to take. The reply stated that "the great sovereigns, having read your indictment of Ivan Samoilovich, and having learnt that he is unacceptable to the Cossack officers and the whole of the Little Russian host, order that he be dismissed from office."[30] Hasty preparations were made for an election. On July 22 Samoilovich was summarily deposed and on the 25th Ivan Mazepa, a member of the Cossack hierarchy, was elected hetman with Golitsyn's support.[31] Mazepa expressed his gratitude by presenting his "benefactor" with a gift of 10,000 rubles.[32]

Although everything had been carried out with the government's approval, Golitsyn was still anxious about reaction in Moscow to the Samoilovich affair. He wrote to Shaklovity: "The case could not have been conducted in a more proper fashion... If anyone voices any objections, I leave it to God to decide; he can judge who is right. We should have expected people to praise God and be thankful to us for the fact that the whole affair was conducted without resistance, bloodshed or confusion."[33] Golitsyn's uneasiness about his position at the start of the campaign had naturally intensified now that he was returning empty-handed, without even a modest victory to report. There were even rumors that the prince himself had started the fire on the steppe, or at least condoned the plan, in order to give himself an excuse for returning to the capital, but there is no evidence of such dishonorable behavior.[34]

The most constructive result of the campaign was the decision to strengthen defence and supply lines in the south by building a fort at the confluence of the Samara and Dniepr rivers, to be named Bogoroditskoe. After the disposal of Samoilovich, who was exiled to Tobol'sk, the armies continued their march northwards and Golitsyn arrived back in Moscow according to the Swedish resident Von Kochen, on the evening of September 4.[35] It might be imagined that the prince returned in disgrace, or at least with little hope of receiving the honors usually granted to a military victor, but nothing could be further from the truth. Sophia had prepared a lavish face-saving exercise in which the undistinguished manoeuvers on the burnt-out steppe were passed off as a resounding victory. A proclamation of September 5 stated: "And you... went to the appointed places with great speed, and reaching those places, the regiments of the great sovereigns' men-at-arms were mobilised with great speed and, adopting military formation, you left those places for the Muslim enemies in the very early springtide, and along the road with your baggage trains towards their Muslim encampment you went with commendable zeal and fervent effort and avid solicitude, and were the whole time engaged in unceasing labors of war, always carrying out unceasingly and with untiring dilligence the sovereigns' military operations; and you gave yourself no rest in caring for the well-being of your regiments and defence from the enemy, and in such a vigorous and zealous manner you crossed many steppe rivers and came within sight of the Crimean settlements... And as you crossed the River Konskaia and went towards the rivers Anchakrak and Karachakrak, the Crimean khan, hearing of your skilful advance with so many troops and of your operations against him, mindful of his helplessness, burned all the steppe around Perekop and the Dniepr in order to escape from the advance of you and your regiments. And seeing you and the men-at-arms of the great sovereigns' regiments advancing, the khan and his Tatars were seized by fear and terror and cast off their usual boldness; he did not appear himself, nor did his Tatar encampments come out to meet you, nowhere did they show themselves and they did not engage you ... in battle, but fallen into the depths of despair they departed for their distant settlements beyond Perekop and other places."[36]

Apart from the exaggeratedly admiring tone, this and other documents contain factual errors, for example in the references to "speedy mobilization" and departure in "very early springtide". The mention of "unceasing labors of war" is difficult to justify, nor could the alleged despair of the khan and his hordes be verified. It is interesting, too, that the charges against the Cossacks were now forgotten and the Tatars were again blamed for starting the fires.

Sophia's expressions of gratitude were not confined to words. Already in August an official had been dispatched to the camp on the River Merl bearing rewards of gold medallions for the officers. Golitsyn received a medal on a gold chain inset with a precious stone and valued, according to Gordon, at 300 ducats;

Gordon's was worth 5.[37] The medals bore portraits of the tsars on one side and Sophia on the reverse.[38] Another source mentions that Golitsyn also received a mace and a sword.[39] Back in Moscow the prince was awarded 300 chervontsy, the conventional cup and robes and 1,000 peasant households,[40] and in addition another cup, robe and 250 rubles for conducting the Samoilovich case "without any detriment or hinderance to the great sovereigns and without any bloodshed or loss of life."[41]

Golitsyn, it appears, still had some thought for the advancement of others. Lefort reports that in an audience with the tsars the prince recommended that he, Lefort, and fellow officers should be promoted, "for they never deserted me and have served Your Majesties faithfully."[42] Writes Lefort: "Prince Vasily Golitsyn spoke on our behalf and I can assure you his generosity was great." A few days later Golitsyn personally conveyed the news that Lefort had been promoted to colonel. He also imparted this fact in a letter to the senators of the Genevan republic, informing them of Lefort's promotion "for his loyal, praiseworthy and valient services" and predicted future advancement and fame.[43]

Despite official recognition of the campaign's "success", others took a less enthusiastic view. King John of Poland in a letter of August 28 to Cardinal Barberini, complained that the Russians had jeopardized the whole allied operation by scarcely moving beyond the Dniepr. They had failed to honor their undertaking to invade the Crimea: "Your Excellency should consider the roguery of these people who, while informing us through their couriers of their military operations in letters full of fine phrases, at the same time desert their posts, sending us little or no information."[44] In Moscow, too, Golitsyn's enemies were not taken in by official eulogies; there were reports that some 40,-50,000 men had been lost.[45]

It is doubtful whether much personal blame can be attached to Golitsyn for the failure of the campaign. Even an experienced soldier such as Gordon had underestimated the difficulties, especially the adverse climatic conditions and activities of arsonists, be they Cossacks or Tatars, which had made progress impossible. The lack of convenient supply bases, the heavy, unwieldy baggage trains and slow-moving troop formations made operations especially hazardous on barren terrain so close to the Tatars' own encampments. The Russians had at least attempted to honor their agreement with the Poles at considerable expense and effort, and could not, in the final analysis, be blamed for the fact that the Tatars had failed to engage them in pitched battle.

Whatever his share of the blame, Golitsyn succeeded in weathering the storm of both just and unjust criticism. Von Kochen reported: "He is still in his former position of honor and stands at the helm of government; in addition Tsarevna Sophia, who wields almost complete control over the administration of the kingdom, supports him strongly."[46] Upon his return the prince resumed his former round of public and private duties. On October 2 a new church was consecrated on his estate of Medvedkovo and on the same day Gordon accompanied him on a visit to the royal village of Izmailovo.[47] On October 4 Sophia and Ivan visited the new church. Not long after this Golitsyn received a gift from the tsarevna. In February an order had been placed for "a wooden bed, of the finest workmanship, which should be more elegant and excellent in its form than all previous beds." A team of craftsmen worked on the bed and its trappings, no expense being spared in the choice of materials, and on October 8 Sophia (the tsars' names appeared in the official rescript) ordered that "the great carved bed be given to Prince Vasily Vasilievich Golitsyn free of charge."[48] On October 26 a son, Mikhail, probably Golitsyn's first grandchild, was born to the wife of the prince's son Aleksei, the baptism taking place on November 6.[49] On November 26 Gordon accompanied Golitsyn to inspect two newly cast cannon. Gordon told the prince of a scheme he had for casting two cannon which would fire missiles horizontally and Golitsyn was sufficiently interested in the idea to ask the Scot to construct a model.[50] The remainder of the year seems to have been spent quietly, with Gordon as practically our only witness, with a visit to the St. Savva Monastery at the end of November and yet another meeting with Gordon at Chernaia Griaz' in mid-December.[51]

1688 was less eventful than its predecessor. As Von Kochen reports in April: "Up until now everything has been quiet in public life and not the slightest disturbance is perceptible. The government is in status quo ante."[52] Work on Golitsyn's Moscow mansion was nearing completion, but the prince spent much of his time outside the city. On January 4 Gordon was received at Medvedkovo and reports that on January 13 the prince journeyed into the countryside.[53] On March 8 he made a pilgrimage to the Monastery of St. Nicholas at Zaraisk. In the same month meetings were held with Polish envoys to discuss the continuation of the war with Turkey. Neither side succeeded in making its intentions clear and the Poles expressed their lack of confidence in the Russians.[54] Another diplomatic venture of that year involved the confirmation of friendly relations with the Venetian republic, one of Poland's allies

against the Turks. In September Ioanniky Likhud, one of
the brothers who had come to Moscow to teach in the new
Slavonic-Greek-Latin Academy and who had gone to Italy
to visit his children, wrote to Golitsyn requesting
accreditation as ambassador.[55]

Golitsyn generally appeared at his most impressive
in personal dealings with foreign envoys and travel-
ers. That useful informant Von Kochen recorded a favorable impression of a meeting he had with the prince in
May: "He was very polite and kind and promised to send
a favorable reply [to a request from the Swedish king];
he also spoke well of the government of His Majesty the
King... He expressed his willingness to give the most
friendly attention to the Swedish crown and assured me
that he always presented everything concerning Sweden
to Their Majesties the Tsars in the most positive
light."[56]

There were also less civilised encounters. The
activities of the dissenters in the south were still
being monitored by the Foreign Office and Golitsyn
seems to have participated actively in investigations;
in this respect his allegiance to the Russian Orthodox
Church was unwavering. In January 1688 Samoil, an Old
Believer priest under arrest in the chancellery, escaped but was recaptured and returned to Golitsyn in person.[57] On March 2 a Don Cossack turned up demanding an
audience with the prince, at which he privately handed
over a number of written denunciations of dissenters.[58]
Shortly afterwards a number of dissenters were interrogated under torture and Golitsyn in person delivered
reports of their confessions to Sophia at Preobrazhenskoe.[59] On May 2 the unfortunate Samoil was tortured in
front of an audience consisting of Golitsyn, his son
Aleksei and other chancellery officials.[60] Such proceedings may seem unedifying, but Golitsyn, who was un-
sympathetic towards the Old Believer cause, would have
been far in advance of his time and would have risked
the castigation of the Church authorities had he
expressed distaste for the conventional methods of
interrogation. Numerous dispatches came from the south,
amongst them expressions of thanks from local leaders
for Golitsyn's firm handling of the dissenters. The
Cossacks were well aware of the prince's authority and
attempted to curry favor and win his patronage. One
Semenov, for example, appealed for compensation for
losses in a recent fire, whilst in another letter a
Cossack referred to himself as "wretched slave" and to
Golitsyn as "father to the poor" in his request for
aid.[61]

The summer months saw numerous visits to country
estates and monasteries, the usual round of Muscovite
court life. On June 16 Golitsyn was at Izmailovo, where

Patrick Gordon lunched with him,[62] very possibly to inspect the work, carried out by the Foreign Office's own architectural team, on a new church which had been commissioned by Sophia in the most up-to-the minute style. It was consecrated in October.[63] On June 28 Tsar Ivan's name-day celebrations were attended by all the boyars, who were entertained with vodka.[64] About a month later the tsar and Sophia dined with the prince at Chernaia Griaz' and the next day a party of boyars was entertained.[65] In the middle of August Golitsyn went to the Trinity Monastery, and on August 30 we find him at Kolomenskoe, where an overdinner conversation with Gordon turned to the topic of England. Golitsyn is reported to have said: "Wee could agree well enough with your King's father and brother, but we cannot come to right with this; he is proud beyond all measure." Presuming that Golitsyn was peeved by the lack of correspondence from the king, Gordon replied "that the King, because of his great troubles in his own dominions, has not leasure to think of business lying so farr off..." to which Golitsyn replied "that the English could not subsist without such [Russian] commodities as leather, hempe, potash, tallow and masts." Gordon gave a "dubious complying answer."[66] England was not one of Golitsyn's main areas of interest or competence, nor of any direct significance for the war with Turkey, so it is perhaps not surprising that the prince was out of touch with the situation there. If anything, his remark is redolent of the often observed Muscovite superiority complex about foreign powers.

The brief respite of the earlier part of 1688 was brought to a close in September by the proclamation of a new campaign against the Tatars.[67] Turkey appeared to be in a weaker position than in 1687, having suffered defeats in Hungary and Dalmatia and also internal disturbances. The proclamation made reference to this: "The Lord God is inflicting severe punishment upon the Turkish state and Muslim rule is about to meet its doom. The Turks have been rendered weak and powerless by the Christian armies and by internecine strife; never before have they suffered such ruin and destruction, never was there such confusion."[68] Russia's campaign was, as before, to be directed against the sultan's vassal, the Crimean khan. Shortly after this announcement Golitsyn made another trip to the Trinity Monastery, no doubt to pray for better luck, and on September 29 we find him dining at the home of foreign merchant Elias Tabert to whom, it will be recalled, he had granted a licence for the manufacture of cloth.[69]

According to Gordon, the commanders for the new campaign were announced on October 28, followed by a new tax levy on merchants and townspeople to finance

the operation.[70] Once again Golitsyn was to act as
commander-in-chief. At about this time news reached
Moscow of the capture of Belgrade by the Emperor of
Austria and rumors began to circulate about the possibility of a separate peace between Turkey and Russia's
allies. An envoy was sent off to Vienna with a list of
Russian demands for inclusion in any forthcoming treaty. If authentic (the historian Brückner, for one,
questions whether they ever existed)[72] they show a
marked lack of realism on the part of Russia and, presumably, Golitsyn. They included a demand for the cession of the whole Crimea (evacuated of Tatars), Azov,
Kazykermen, Ochakov and other towns to Russia, the
release of all prisoners of war without compensation
and payment of two million gold crowns to the tsars.[72]
These requirements were ambitious in the extreme in the
absence of Russian victories over the Tatars and the
territorial claims were achieved only by an altogether
stronger Russia during the reign of Catherine the
Great.

On November 23 Golitsyn accompanied Tsar Peter to
the St. Savva Monastery, one of the few recorded occasions on which he personally attended the younger tsar,
and on the 31st Ivan and Sophia also arrived. On December 8 Gordon dined with him and was again questioned
about England.[73]

No contemporary records survive to tell us what
opinion, if any, the younger tsar had of his sister's
chief minister at this stage of the regency, but it was
becoming evident that Sophia's position, and hence that
of Golitsyn, was becoming more precarious. Peter, a
mere child when the regency began, was fast approaching
maturity and being encouraged by his supporters to take
a greater interest in his responsibilities. Late in
1687 Von Kochen had reported to his government that
"the prime minister Prince Golitsyn is now obliged to
report to His Royal Majesty on all important matters,
which never happened previously."[74] In January 1688
Peter paid his first visit to the boyar duma,[75] and in
May L.K. Naryshkin and T.N. Streshnev were raised to
the rank of boyar at the tsar's recommendation.[76] In
March 1688 Peter visited the Foreign Office in Golitsyn's absence, accompanied by about 20 retainers. Chancellery clerks reported the visit to Golitsyn and his
son: "We wish to inform you, sires, that on this 16th
day of March the great sovereigns, their royal majesties, attended a requiem for the dead in the Archangel
Cathedral and afterwards in the fourth hour of the
night the great sovereign and grand prince Peter Alekseevich ... paid a visit to the state ambassadorial
chancellery and was pleased to pause at the table in
the great reception chamber and to inspect the list of

detainees and deigned also to visit the secret treasure store and inspect the icons." They listed his attendants, who included Golitsyn's "enemy" of 1687 Prince M.A. Cherkassky and his cousin Boris Golitsyn, one of Peter's closest advisers.[77] The sensitive prince could not have been pleased by this unannounced visit which had all the signs of being a "spying" exercise engineered by some of his opponents in the younger tsar's camp. In September 1688 he reacted with annoyance to Peter's request for the requisition of five drummers and five pipers from Gordon's regiment, but was obliged to comply.[78] Did the prince suspect, one wonders, that the "play" regiments at Preobrazhenskoe were fast becoming more than mere toys? Perhaps even more significant, on January 27, 1689 the end of Peter's boyhood was marked by his marriage to Evdokiia Feodorovna Lopukhina, a Russian girl of good family.[79] Ivan's marriage had so far failed to produce a male heir and it now seemed possible that Peter would beat him to it, despite his evident lack of interest in his new bride, who had been selected by his mother and her circle who were, of course, fully aware of the marriage's political implications. Despite all these ominous signs, however, Peter at this stage was in no particular haste to devote himself to affairs of state and Golitsyn could have found some comfort in the tsar's inconsistent attitude towards his responsibilities. In April 1689 the future founder of the Russian navy was on Lake Pereslavl' indulging in his love of sailing boats, leaving the reins of government once again entirely in the hands of Sophia and her advisers.

A useful analysis of Golitsyn's position is provided by the French Jesuit Father Philippe Avril (1654-98) who arrived in Moscow in January 1689 with his companion Father Beauvollier bearing a letter of recommendation from the King of France and requesting safe passage to China: "We entreat you to grant those Fathers all such permission and passports as they shall have occasion for, not only to pass and repass through these Territories and Seas that are under your Command, but also there, to receive all manner of Protection and Assistance."[81] Their arrival had been preceded by a letter from the Marquis de Béthune, the French attaché in Warsaw, addressed to Golitsyn and reminding him of "the obliging manner wherewith Your Highness receiv'd the two Missionaries that return'd from Persia last year", and requesting instructions about any special formalities that the Jesuits should comply with before leaving for Moscow, but the letter was not answered.[82]

Golitsyn's silence and difficulties at the border, which they eventually succeeded in crossing disguised as chaplains to a Polish diplomat, boded ill for the

59

Jesuits. Avril had already met Golitsyn when he visited Moscow en route for Astrakhan in 1685. On that occasion the prince had greeted him warmly and "testifi'd a great kindness for us, and assur'd us of all the Services that could be expected from him."[83] Naturally, on his second visit Avril again applied to Golitsyn and was received "with all manner of Civility" and given an apology for the ill-treatment they had received.[84] The Jesuit left a flattering assessment of Golitsyn's character: "The first Minister of State, who was of the Illustrious Race of the Jagellons, was undoubtedly the most accomplish'd and knowing Lord at the Court of Moscow, he lov'd Strangers, and particularly the French, because the Noble Sentiments he had observ'd in them, were very consonant to his own; for which reason, it was rumour'd that his Heart was as much French as his Name. It was no fault of his, that we did not receive all the satisfaction he made us hope for, the first time we had the honour to speak to him; and had he been absolute Master, and not oblig'd to keep great Measures with all the Boyars who were concern'd in the management of Affairs, he would willingly have granted us the Passage of Siberia, and have facilitated our entrance into China, out of respect to Lewis le Grand, whose Admirer he was, to that degree, that I have often been told that he caus'd his Son to wear his Majestie's Picture in the form of a Cross of Maltha."[85]

The presence of the Jesuits in Moscow was strongly resented by the patriarch whose unfriendly relations with Golitsyn had been worstened by the arrival of Jesuits in 1684 in fulfilment of the prince's agreement with Austria. As Georgius David wrote: "Since our arrival the patriarch has not uttered one friendly word to Prince Golitsyn, because he was convinced that we had been received in Moscow to bring about the union of the churches. When my companion arrived, the patriarch is alleged to have exclaimed with sighs and tears: 'After my death all Moscow will fall into the hands of the Jesuits'."[86] In Avril's opinion Golitsyn was also dissuaded from intervening on his behalf by two "vexatious accidents" -- one an assassination attempt when he was driving to the palace in his sleigh. The would-be assassin was overpowered by the prince's attendants but had time to shout: "Infamous Tyrant ... since I have been so unfortunate as to fail in this attempt, to deliver my Country from the most horrid Monster, that ever bred in it, by making thee a Sacrifice, know that some happier hand than mine will be found, and that among upwards of three hundred Citizens, who pitty the People, that it daily oppress'd by thee, some will take better measures that I have done."[87] In the second incident a coffin was discovered outside the gates of

Golitsyn's mansion inscribed with the warning that "unless the Campaign that art going to open, prove more successful than the former, thou can'st not avoid this."88 Both these events must have disturbed the sensitive Golitsyn, who set much store by public opinion. Denunciations of him as a "monster" and "oppressor of the people" were patently absurd and are not reflected in other contemporary sources, but the reference to his military failure in the south must have struck a strong chord. Other circumstances also influenced the prince's treatment of the Jesuits. For a start, relations with the King of France, the Jesuits' patron, had been damaged by French mistreatment of Russian ambassadors on a mission in 1687 and, as luck would have it, Avril's arrival in Moscow coincided with that of the envoy from Protestant Brandenburg who sought, amongst other things, to persuade the tsars to offer sanctuary to Huguenots. A decree offering right of entry and protection for the religious exiles was issued on January 18, along with two trade agreements.89 The Brandenburg envoys were thus in a convenient position to remind the Russians of the humiliation of their representatives by the French and on January 31 the Jesuits were ordered to leave Moscow on the grounds that the king's letter contained wrongly formulated titles and because of the mistreatment of Dolgoruky and Myshetsky in 1687.90 Avril believed that Golitsyn opposed this decision: "The truth is, that, had he been minded to make use of his own Authority on that occasion, he might easily have obtain'ed from the Czars, the revocation of the Orders we have mention'd. But having already too many Enemies against him, he was oblig'd to sacrifice us, for fear of imbroiling himself the more, and of being involv'd into more troubles than he daily met with already, notwithstanding the high Post he possess'd, which was not capable to secure him from the Shaft[s of] Envy. We were very sensible, at that very time when he labour'd to obtain the favour we desir'd, he had a great deal of reason to behave himself prudently towards everybody, and not to take too much advantage of the Credit he deriv'd from his Place of Prime Minister, nor of the consideration the Eldest of the Czars express'd for him, as well as the Princess Sophia, whose Creature he was."91

It was Avril's French connections rather than his religious affiliation that sealed his fate, for in February 1689 the Jesuit Father Tobias Tichavsky was admitted to Moscow to join Father David in the Foreign Colony, with credentials from the Emperor of Austria.92 Similarly in January 1689 two other Jesuits, Zapolski and Terpilowski, had arrived bound for China with the backing of Russia's ally the King of Poland and were allowed to proceed to Astrakhan.[93] Nevertheless, Golitsyn felt constrained to behave differently towards the French Jesuits because of the growing sense of insecurity which Avril analyses so clearly.

The new campaign in the Crimea was imminent. It was planned that the second attempt should begin earlier in order to avoid the worst of the summer heat and the threat of bush fires. According to Gordon, Golitsyn departed for the Trinity Monastery on January 28, two days after the wedding of his daughter Irina to Prince Odoevsky, a pilgrimage which he had also made shortly before the start of the first campaign. He returned on February 7.[94] Gordon left for the south on February 12 and it can be assumed that Golitsyn left around the same date. On March 6 he met up with the Scot and fellow officers near the town of Sumy and dined in the town, and on the 8th Gordon had a consultation with the prince.[95]

First-hand accounts of the events which followed can be found in Golitsyn's own war dispatches and Gordon's diaries. De la Neuville supplies a second-hand report. On March 19 Golitsyn arrived in Akhtyrka and discovered that Hetman Mazepa's army had left the hetman's capital Baturin on the 17th.[96] Progress beyond Akhtyrka was delayed by "great cold and snows" and by the non-arrival of pay for the troops. On March 27 they arrived at Krasny Kut on the River Merl, but found that the bridge had been swept away by floods so that the crossing had to be improvised. By April 13 they had advanced as far as the Orel River, where they were joined by B.P. Sheremet'ev's regiment. April 15 brought a dispatch from the court with news of the birth of a daughter, Maria, to Tsar Ivan's wife, for which Golitsyn ordered prayers of thanksgiving to be said despite probable disappointment that the child was not a son. The crossing of the Orel river caused further difficulties. In addition to the many streams to be crossed the pace of the armies was slowed down by the cumbersome supplies carried by the soldiers and by the heavy artillery of some 700 guns. Later some of the horses escaped to cause further delay.[97] On April 20 Golitsyn met Mazepa at the new fortress of Bogoroditskoe. The march proceeded, but on April 26 Golitsyn referred to a problem which had often dogged Muscovite campaigns -- the non-arrival or slow mobilization of military servitors. By May 3 they had reached the furthest limit of the 1687 march, the River Karachakrak, and set off into "unexplored" terrain. The first Tatar captives were brought in on the following day. On May 12, when they reckoned to be within four days' march of Perekop, the Tatars made their first appearance and on May 15 they attacked.

Golitsyn's dispatches and subsequent official accounts based on them portray the Russian action in a heroic light. The battles, he wrote, raged from two until ten, the Russian troops fighting "with the infidels courageously and boldly; and they killed many renowned Tatar nobles and officers and many rank-and-file soldiers and took many alive, and captured banners, horses and many items of equipment, and the captured men were interrogated by us and said that a large number of their fellows were killed and wounded."[98] Gordon reports, less partially, that "there were dead and wounded on both sides, and the Russians took some prisoners. When the Russians made their second attack the enemy rushed off at full gallop towards Kazykermen." He mentions "crush, disorder and disobedience" in the Russian ranks.[99] In De la Neuville's version, allegedly obtained from the Polish resident in Moscow, there were incidences of outright cowardice on the Russian side. Emel'ian Ukraintsev, for example, who was "ignorant of the art of warfare and in that a veritable Muscovite" was said to be so terrified that he offered no resistance to the Tatars. The enemy is said to have captured many Russian guns.[100]

On May 16 there was another encounter with the khan, who "with all his aforementioned hordes engaged us in a mighty and fierce battle for the whole day.. And those infidels were repelled and driven from the battle field in a bloody engagement by the courage and valor of the great sovereigns' men-at-arms, and they were forced to quit the battle field in which they had made persistent and savage attacks upon us." The next day the khan attacked again and then withdrew to Perekop. Golitsyn was quick to send off news of the three-day engagement -- the first major encounter of both campaigns -- to the King of Poland, referring to "the glorious victory which the All Highest has granted to his Christian people, oppressed these hundred years past, over their arch-enemy the Tatars." He claimed that the khan had left 30,000 troops dead and wounded, including his son, on the field of battle, and that 200 nobles had been captured and sent to Moscow.[101]

On May 20 Golitsyn reached Perekop, the fortress guarding the approaches to the Crimean peninsula. "We reconnoitered to see where we might entrench ourselves and also where we might obtain water and food for the great sovereigns' men-at-arms, but our investigations and also those of your subject Ivan Stepanovich Mazepa... revealed that there was nowhere to obtain horse fodder; from Kalanchak everything was trampled down and stamped out and there was also no water to be had. On the right side beneath the very walls of Perekop was the Black Sea, on the left side the Putrid Lake, in

63

which there is salt water, and between these the baggage trains of your slaves were stationed."[102]

According to Golitsyn, the khan remained ensconced in Perekop having burnt the outlying districts. Several times Tatar officials came out with offers of peace based on the terms of the treaty of 1681, but Golitsyn replied that his men would be willing to "fight and shed their blood" were it not for the shortage of food and water. On May 21 Golitsyn took the decision to retreat, having spurned the khan's offers of a settlement. They had been without supplies of fresh water for eight days and "if we had remained in Perekop another day it would have been impossible to lead out the great sovereigns' men-at-arms without, God preserve us, great and terrible losses." They arrived safely at the Belozerka river on June 1 having been spared any serious attempts at pursuit, although there were some minor encounters with Belgorod Tatars and Turks. On June 11 (14th according to Gordon) they arrived back at Bogoroditskoe.[103] Shortly afterwards a band of Tatars attacked men cutting grass and prisoners taken in the ensuing squirmish reported, amongst other things, that the Crimeans had been intimidated at the size of the tsars' armies ("no-one expected that they would have to face such troops") and that the khan had ordered what amounted to a mass evacuation in the path of the enemy.[104]

Zheliabuzhsky, a contemporary of Golitsyn's, alleged that the prince took care to ensure that all reports of the campaign tallied with his own, ordering officers "to write in their statements that it was impossible to march on Perekop because in Perekop there was no water or food" whereas in reality, Zheliabuzhsky claimed, Golitsyn was induced to retreat by a bribe of two barrels of gold from the khan.[105] These inducements turned out to be mere brass concealed beneath a thin gold layer. De la Neuville gives another version of the Perekop affair, according to which Golitsyn demanded of the khan that all Russian prisoners-of-war be released, that there be no further raids on the tsars' territory and that the khan renounce all claim to tribute, leave the Poles in peace and withdraw his aid to Turkey. The khan's response to demands which Golitsyn was in no position to enforce was a counter-demand for 240,000 écus of unpaid tribute.[106] Other alleged evidence of Golitsyn's treachery at Perekop was later produced during the trial of Fedor Shaklovity in September 1689. A Cossack by the name of Evstafy Glistin, who had been a prisoner of the Tatars, reported that the prince was bribed with two barrels of gold pieces and that the khan ordered the preparation of a further fifteen "fake" barrels filled with tar with a layer of gold at each end.[107] Much of Glistin's testimony was highly suspect and, like much of the evidence produced against Sophia's party after her downfall, carries little weight. Schleissing also gives a somewhat garbled account of rumors originating in both the first and second Crimean campaigns to the effect that Golitsyn was bribed with "French gold" to sabotage the war. He remarks wryly that "one could sooner believe that the heavens had fallen in and the high mountains rolled away, than that this universally loved Golitsyn should have let himself be led into this falsehood... But such must be the potency of French gold that it can capture and bewitch even the most steadfast and intrepid natures."[108]

Whatever the truth of these rumors, the fact remains that Perekop was not taken and the Crimea beyond it was unconquered. Despite reports of Russian heroism and Tatar panic in official dispatches, there was little to show for the campaign, especially if one accepts Lefort's estimate, in a letter to a relative, of as many as 20,000 Russians killed, 15,000 captured and 70 cannon and most of the supplies lost.[109] On the way home, on June 29, the armies rested on SS. Peter and Paul day. This was also Tsar Peter's name day, but Gordon reports that it was not marked by any special celebrations.[110]

Anyone who had access only to Golitsyn's reports and the proclamations later issued by Sophia may be forgiven for thinking that a great victory had been won. A rescript of praise, addressed to Golitsyn on June 19 in the name of the tsars, stated: "We, the great sovereigns, give our most gracious thanks to you, our own boyar and guardian, for your great and devoted service. By your efforts those savage and inveterate foes of the Holy Cross and all Christendom have been crushed and defeated and scattered by our royal armies in their infidel abode, an event quite unprecedented. They destroyed their own dwellings, their customary savage impudence deserted them, they were seized with terror and despair and set fire to the outskirts, villages and hamlets around Perekop. They did not venture out of Perekop with their infidel hordes to meet you and did not engage you as you retreated. And now you have returned in safety to our frontiers with all the men-at-arms after winning the aforementioned victories, famed throughout the world."[111] A similarly glowing report was included in a rescript of thanksgiving sent to the Trinity Monastery on June 15 with rewards for the monks' prayers of intercession.[112]

The armies arrived back in Moscow in the middle of July. On the 19th Golitsyn was greeted at the city's Serpukhov gates by Sophia, who had spent the morning in prayers and come out ostensibly to attend the reception of the icons and crosses that had been carried during the campaign. In the procession into the center of Moscow Sophia rode with Golitsyn and other generals behind the icons and they were met in the Kremlin by Tsar Ivan and Patriarch Joachim, who conducted a service of thanksgiving. This was followed by a reception at the palace where a state secretary read out a speech of welcome to the "returning heroes".113 Peter was absent from these ceremonies for reasons which were soon to become apparent.

Sophia was intent, as after the first campaign, on convincing the public that a victory had been won. It is even possible that she genuinely believed in her own propaganda. Her only surviving personal letters to Golitsyn show the extent of her self-deception and, incidently, provide one of the few pieces of direct evidence for the nature of the relationship between the tsarevna and her chief minister. In response to news of one of the "victories" outside Perekop she assured the prince: "You have fully earned prosperity since, by the grace of God and the Blessed Virgin and by your own wisdom and good fortune, you have triumphed over the Hagarite."114 In a second letter, written after the retreat from Perekop, she writes: "My lord and light and hope, may you have long life and prosperity! Joyful indeed is this day on which the Lord God has glorified his Holy Name and the name of his mother the Blessed Virgin. The like of his divine mercy has not been heard of throughout the ages, nor have our forefathers related it: God has delivered you, my dear, as once he delivered the Israelites out of the land of Egypt through his saint Moses. Praise be to God for the mercy he has shown us through you! My lord, how can I ever repay you for your innumerable labors? My joy, light of my eyes, I cannot believe that I shall see you again. Great indeed will be the day when you are with me again, my dear. If it were only possible I would have you before me every single day. Your letters, in God's safekeeping, have all reached me safely from Perekop... On the 11th five dispatches arrived from Perekop. I was strolling in the vicinity of Vozdvizhenskoe and had just reached the Monastery of St. Sergius the Miracle Worker when at the main gates I received your battle reports. I cannot remember how I entered; I read as I walked along. How can I ever express my thanks to God and to his mother the Blessed Virgin and to the gracious worker of miracles St. Sergius for their mercy?... I have carried out all your instructions about visiting monasteries and have visited them all on foot. Soon I shall send you Vasily Narbekov with the delivery, but the gold pieces are not yet ready. Do not grieve on their account; it would be a pity to delay you. They will be ready soon and I shall send them at once. I am also sending the strel'tsy money and will send it as soon as it is ready. Tell them that it will be sent. Your devotion, my dear, will be rewarded... You write my dear, that I should pray for you. God knows how much I long to see you again, my dear, and I trust in his mercy that he will allow me to see you, my hope. Deal with the troops as you yourself have written, as you think fit. And I, my lord, am well, thanks to your prayers; we are all well. When God willing, I see you, my light, I shall tell you everything that had happened. Do not tarry, my light; continue your march gradually, for you have toiled so much. How can I ever repay you, my light, for your great service and for all your labors? If you had not toiled so much, no-one else would have done so."[115]

The blend of piety, devotion and practicality in these letters is striking and Sophia had no difficulty in solving her rhetorical problem about "repayment". On July 23 Golitsyn, Sophia and courtiers attended prayers of thanksgiving at the Novedevichy Convent, after which vodka was distributed,[116] and on July 25 leave from chancellery duties was granted to participants in the campaign until January 6.[117] A further proclamation, read out to boyars in an antechamber of the palace on July 24, listed honors and rewards. In an account of the campaign, very similarly worded to official accounts of the campaign of 1687, the audience learned of how the tsars's armies approached the Tatar settlements in the spring and how, on May 15-18, there were "great and fierce" battles when all the strength of the infidel warriors was thrown into the fray, "but the Russian armies fought with these infidels valiantly and courageously... and those Muselmans left the battlefields with great losses and ran off from the final battle once and for all into the Crimea."[118] The khan was made out to be cowed and intimidated by the Russian advance, offering peace terms which proved uncongenial to the Russians who were prevented from pushing home their advantage only by lack of fodder and water. For his "loyal and zealous service and fervent and unceasing endeavor in that military encounter... for the glorious and splendid victory over the infidel" Golitsyn was awarded a gold cup, a sable-lined kaftan of cloth-of-gold, a salary supplement of 300 rubles and a hereditary estate of 1,500 souls in Suzdal'.[119] Other officers received gifts commensurate with their rank, and compensatory payments were made for wounds received during the battles.[120]

Not everyone shared Sophia's enthusiam. As De la Neuville tells us: "Upon his return to Moscow Prince Golitsyn found that things were not as he hoped. His

enemies, having ascertained the truth about his campaign, had made him hateful to Tsar Peter."[121] Peter,
it will be recalled, did not attend the reception on
July 15, nor did he appear at the nameday celebrations
of his great-aunt Tsarevna Anna Mikhailovna on July
25. Gordon records that on July 24 Peter withheld permission for the distribution of rewards and was persuaded only with difficulty to allow the ceremony on the
27th to go ahead.[122] Peter was especially reluctant to
receive the "returning hero" and on July 24 he refused
to grant an audience to Golitsyn and fellow officers
who wished to thank him for the rewards, ostensibly
issued in the joint name of the tsars.[123] There were
even rumors that Peter had initially refused to return
to Moscow until Golitsyn had been arrested.[124] An "open
eruption or breach", comments Gordon, had now occurred
between the opposing court factions.[125] There had been
earlier signs of the growing tension between Peter and
Sophia. On July 8 during a ceremony in the Cathedral of
Our Lady of Kazan' in commemoration of the liberation
of Moscow in 1612, at which Sophia played her by now
prominent and public part, Peter had angrily accused
her of flouting convention and rising above her station
and ordered her to leave. When she refused, the tsar
himself left Moscow in a rage.[126]

Peter's condemnation of the Crimean campaign may,
in retrospect, seem almost as unjustified and partial
as Sophia's enthusiam. Soviet historians have generally
taken a lenient, although by no means eulogistic view
of Golitsyn's efforts, regarding the two campaign as
essential elements in the wider "Crimean question"
which was to be resolved only in the reign of Catherine
II. Outright victory, it has been argued, was not to be
expected. The campaigns were, nonetheless, undertaken
for "serious economic and political reasons" and were
of strategic importance to Russia's allies, relieving
pressure by depriving the Turks of Tatar aid, immobi-
lising enemy reinforcements (e.g. the Belgorod Tatars)
and generally augmenting the allies' show of strength
against Turkey.[127] In the summer of 1689, however, it
was difficult to take such a generous view in the face
of reports of heavy casualties and rumors of bribery
and corruption at the walls of Perekop. This and the
obvious absence of any positive territorial or political gains provided ample ammunition for Golitsyn's opponents.

# CHAPTER FIVE

## DISGRACE AND EXILE

In the middle of August 1689 a foreigner arrived
in Moscow who was to provide one of the most detailed
and dramatic surviving accounts of the political events
then unfolding in the capital. Foy de la Neuville, who
has been extensively quoted on previous occasions,
claimed to have been sent to Russia by François-Gaston,
Marquis de Béthune, the French attaché in Warsaw, to
investigate Russian relations with Brandenburg and
Sweden. In view of the current hostility towards the
French, he entered Russia as an agent of the King of
Poland, who presented him with credentials on July 1.
On his own evidence, he was in Moscow from mid-August
to mid-December.[1] There has been some debate about De
la Neuville's true identity,[2] but whatever the full
story may be, the writer shows such detailed knowledge
of events of 1689, much of it verified by other contemporary sources (e.g. Gordon's diaries) not published
until much later, that he cannot be ignored. De la
Neuville is, moreover, especially useful for present
purposes as he was a great admirer of Golitsyn, whom he
singled out as a glowing exception amongst a race which
he generally regarded as "suspicious and mistrustful,
cruel, sodomists, gluttons, misers, knaves and cowards,
slaves every one."[3] He was aware of Golitsyn's worsten-
ing position and recounts many rumors, and some speculations of his own, about the schemes of Sophia and her
party for overcoming their enemies and prolonging their
power. His first meeting with the prince took place in
the Foreign Office, and at an audience a few days later
Golitsyn received the Frenchmen "in a manner as to make
me believe that I was at the court of some Italian
prince. During the conversation in Latin on everything
that was taking place in Europe and on my opinion of
the war which the Emperor and a number of princes were
waging with France, and on the revolution in England,
he presented me with various spirits and wines, at the
same time advising me in an obliging manner not to
drink them. He promised to arrange an audience in several days. This he would certainly have done were it not
for his disgrace, which brought about such a great
change in circumstances that one heard cries of fire
and murder; and if fortune had not contrived that Tsar
Peter had the daring to constrain the leaders of the
Princess's party, there would have been a massacre
equal to those of which we spoke earlier." (i.e. the
1682 rebellion)[4]

What were Sophia's plans now that the "open errup-
tion or breach" had occurred and the second Crimean
campaign had failed to provide her regime with the
prestige which it so desperately needed? De la Neuville
is no doubt correct in believing that from the very
beginning of the regency Sophia had anticipated the
challenge that Peter was bound sooner or later to present and had formulated schemes which became more and
more desperate as Peter approached his majority and
showed some signs of wishing to participate actively in
government. At the same time, De la Neuville represented Golitsyn's part in these "schemes" as that of a
moderator, who found plotting uncongenial, an image
which tallies with the prince's behavior during the
rebellion of 1682. De la Neuville reports, for example,
that Sophia initially intended to kill both tsars so
that she and Golitsyn could rule, but the prince "represented to her the horror of this design, persuading
her that the execution could not fail to bring down
upon them universal hatred and indignation."[5] A more
subtle alternative was devised. Children must be
obtained from Tsar Ivan (married, it will be recalled,
in 1684) by presenting his wife with a lover, thereby
weakening the claim of Peter and his prospective heirs
to the throne. Peter would be removed to a monastery or
otherwise "eliminated", after which Ivan would be
forced to repudiate his wife on grounds of adultery,
send her to a covent and Golitsyn and Sophia would
continue to rule. According to De la Neuville, Golitsyn
had additonal plans. Having joined Moscow to Rome, he
would hope to outlive Sophia and then obtain the Pope's
confirmation of his own son's claim to the Muscovite
throne.[6]

De la Neuville evidently based his reports upon
rumor, but there may be an element of truth in some of
these crude schemes. The political usefulness of male
heirs from Tsar Ivan had not escaped Sophia, but by
1689 the plan related by De la Neuville, even if it had
ever existed, was about to be invalidated. Ivan's marriage had produced only a daughter (apparently without
the intervention of specially appointed lovers) and
Peter's wife was already pregnant with her first child,
the ill-fated Aleksei who was born in February 1690.
The rumors of Golitsyn's intended affiliation with Rome
were no doubt partly raised by his known sympathy for
Jesuits, not to mention the accusations of "Latinism"
levelled against certain of Sophia's adherents, such as
the monk Silvester Medvedev. Georgius David relates a
similar rumor that Sophia intended to kill Peter, ele-
vated Golitsyn to the throne then seek unity with
Rome.[7]

The alleged plan to kill Peter is, of course, crucial, for it would have been Sophia's ultimate weapon in extending her regency indefinitely, given that Ivan was incapable of ruling. De la Neuville believes that Golitsyn finally acquiesced to such a deed. "He could not resist all her reasons and, although he was prudent and wise and by nature an enemy of all violent counsels, he no longer opposed her design."8 He reports that the "prudent" Golitsyn had contingency plans in case the intended assassination should misfire-- to send his son Aleksei to Poland with the bulk of their wealth and to follow him there if the need arose.9 The plot to murder Peter remains unproven, although much evidence, generally inconsistent and tangled, was presented at the "trial" of Fedor Shaklkovity and his associates. What is important is that Peter believed that his life was in danger, a conviction that could only be strengthened by the sort of rumors on which De la Neuville based his speculations.

The charge that Golitsyn intended to marry Sophia and send his wife to a convent also exists only in rumor, although later during the investigations that followed Sophia's downfall, a Pole named Silin testified that Silvester Medevedev had told him that the tsarevna wished to marry Golitsyn and replace Patriarch Joachim by himself, Medevedev.10 Such accusations were naturally music to the ears of Peter's followers, but later still, in the 1720s, Prince B.I. Kurakin wrote that Sophia's plans for marrying Golitsyn and ruling jointly with him "were only rumors amongst the people... Everybody knew that this prince Golitsyn was her gallant and therefore anticipated that a wedding would take place shortly."11 Kurakin suggested, moreover, that by 1687 Golitsyn had been partially replaced in Sophia's affections by the "second favorite" (to use Gordon's phrase), Fedor Shaklovity, who "profited much from amorous intrigue with Tsarevna Sophia and enjoyed more of her confidence in these nocturnal pleasures than did Prince Golitsyn, only not so openly."12 De la Neuville, our only source of another rumor, namely that Sophia had children by Golitsyn, believes that pressure for marriage came solely from Sophia. She was eager to exchange her "scandalous commerce with the prince for the sacrament of marriage", but Golitsyn refused to abandon his wife, "being by nature an honorable man. In addition he had received much property from her, and children who were more dear to him than those he had by the princess."13 Certainly Golitsyn's wife Evdok'ia Ivanovna, who had been observed at a reception in the prince's country mansion in 1684 by Laurent Rinhuber, was still alive and well in 1689. She gave birth to her last child, Mikhail, in about 1689 and accompanied her

71

husband into exile in September 1689. If there was any foundation to the rumors of the intimate relationship between the tsarevna and Golitsyn they do not appear to have damaged Evdok'ia's loyalty.

There have been endless speculations on Sophia's plans for removing Peter from power. F.C. Weber, for example, wrote in 1723 that she "did either out of Love to Ivan, or out of a boundless desire of governing try all Methods imaginable to remove out of the Way the present Czar her Brother by the Father's second Marriage, or at least to get him some way or other excluded from the Succession. To compass which End she judged it the surest Method to deprive the young Czar Peter of all Education by letting him carelessly grow up among a Company of raw Youths, in Hopes that by an unbecoming Conduct he would in time render himself odious to the People, and that his promising Genius and the good Sense, of which he gave early Proofs, would be stifled by Debauches and Licentiousness, and consequently he be rendered unfit for Government and great Enterprizes."[14]

The claim that Sophia tried to remove Peter "out of the way" is exaggerated. Peter was never "banned" from Moscow or "exiled" to Preobrazhenskoe. He was frequently in the capital, as demonstrated by records of court ceremonials,[15] and if he took a less active role in state occasions that Ivan this was no doubt of his own volition. As Solov'ev wrote, it was his "flamboyant passionate nature which drove him out of the palace and onto the street."[16] Nor was Peter "deprived" of education, as his surviving school note books and numerous requests for the supply of books and scientific instruments show.[17] If Peter's education was somewhat unorthodox it was because of Peter's own unusual tastes and interests rather than Sophia's deviousness.

The best validated charge against Sophia is that she raised herself on a par with her brothers, creating the impression, without any legal sanction, that she was co-ruler and autocrat in her own right. It is these activities which were emphasized in a letter from Peter to Ivan, written between September 8-12, 1689. Peter wrote that at their coronation "there was no mention that a third person should rule jointly with us. But you yourself are aware of how our sister the tsarevna Sophia Alekseevna chose to rule our state by her own will and that in that rule there was much that was harmful to our own persons and burdensom to the people." Significantly Peter attributes the alleged regicide plot only to Shaklovity and his clique. "And now, sovereign brother, the time has come for both of us ourselves to rule the kingdom entrusted to us by God, since we have come to age, but we cannot allow that

72

third dishonorable person, our sister the tsarevna Sophia Alekseevna to share the titles and the administration with us two male personages... for she chose to interfere in affairs of government and to include herself in titles without our leave and she also wished as a final insult to us to be crowned with the royal crown."[18] There is ample evidence to support these accusations, notably the majority of decrees and rescripts issued from 1686 onwards in which Sophia's name is given autocratic status alongside that of her brothers. In 1687 an envoy in Venice is alleged to have announced that Sophia was "co-ruler" (sotsarstvuet) with Peter and Ivan, and in the same year Sophia commissioned a portrait of herself wearing a crown and bearing a scepter, with the Latin titles "Sofia Alexiovna, Dei Gratia, Augustissima ac Praepotentissima Magna Domina Carevna ac Magna Kniazna totius Magnae, Parvae atque Albae Russiae Autocratix, Moscoviae, Kioviae, Vladimirae etc. etc."[19] In the words of Voltaire: "Sophia enjoyed all the honors of a sovereign; her bust was on the public coin, she signed all dispatches, held the first place in council, and enjoyed a power without control."[20]

Sophia's desire to be crowned was one of the gravest items of evidence against her. In August 1687, it is alleged, she asked Fedora Shaklovity to put the proposal for her coronation to the musketeers. September 1, New Year's Day, was deemed an appropriate date. There was some support for the idea, but many feared the disapproval of Peter, the patriarch and the boyars. When twenty potential supporters came forward to put the plan into action, however, Sophia is said to have changed her mind for fear of her brothers' reaction.[21] In evidence obtained after Golitsyn's exile, additional charges were made. In November 1691, for example, Archimandrite Isaiah of the Monastery of SS. George and Paul on Mount Athos, reported that during a visit to Moscow in 1689 he was summoned by Golitsyn who asked him to obtain the permission of the ecumenical patriarchs for Sophia to be crowned "and to be mentioned together with the great sovereigns in every law."[22] Golitsyn's attitude to Sophia's assumption of the autocratic titles and prerogatives cannot be established with any certainty. It will be recalled that during the campaign of 1687 he showed apprehension when toasting the tsarevna together with the tsars and he cannot be shown to have taken an active part in the intrigue with the musketeers in either 1682 or 1689. In depositions made at the begining of his exile he claimed that he believed the tsars to have approved of Sophia's power, but Peter's strong disapproval, fanned by his advisers, must have been increasingly evident. What is certain is that Golitsyn was loyal to Sophia to whose patronage he owed his position and probably believed that by serving her he was serving the best interests of Russia. His lack of talent for intrigue and manoeuvering made him fail to appreciate and cope with the change in the balance of power, with the result that not until the very end of the events leading up to the tsarevna's overthrow did he desert her camp and obey Peter's summons to all servitors. By then it was too late for a change of allegiance to be accepted.

Leaving aside for a moment the question of the existence of a fully-fledged plot against Peter's life, at the beginning of August 1689 both sides had good reason to fear the other and their fears were increased by the rumors circulating in the capital. After Peter's refusal to receive Golitsyn Sophia left for the Novodevichy Convent, accompanied by a unit of musketeers. She is said to have complained that Tsaritsa Natalia was stirring up trouble against her, exclaiming in tones reminiscent of May 1682: "If you need us, stand by us. If not, we shall leave the country."[23] On August 4 Peter, who was at Izmailovo to celebrate his wife's name-day, received a group of servitors, amongst them Shaklovity. The latter was ordered to hand over one of his musketeers and when he refused was arrested but released shortly afterwards. In a diary entry for August 6 Gordon spoke of rumors "unsafe to be uttered."[24] In the middle of the night of August 7-8 news reached Peter at Preobrazhenskoe that musketeers were gathering in the city with the aim of coming to kill him. He fled to the Trinity Monastery in a panic.[25] It is possible that this "plot" was based on a rumor spread by Peter's own supporters who were eager to precipitate action and deepen the rift between the two sides. There was certainly more musketeer activity than usual in the city on the night in question, but the troops themselves appear to have been brought to the Kremlin by a letter warning them that Peter's "play" regiments were on their way to kill Ivan and his sisters.[26] Both sides were thus put on the alert and open confrontation became inevitable.

As in 1682 Golitsyn's part in the confrontation remains less than clear. One source, musketeer colonel Andrei Normatsky reported that the prince gave the order for all the gates into the Kremlin, Kitaigorod and Belygorod to be closed on August 7 in anticipation of an incident, but Golitsyn later denied all knowledge of musketeer activities on August 7-8. It is recorded elsewhere that Golitsyn was at home sick on that day and was visited by Shaklovity, the man actually in charge of proceedings.[27]

On the 8th it became clear that something of the order of siege preparations were taking place at the Trinity Monastery. Peter's mother, wife and sister, members of the "play" regiments and the tsar's chief adviser Prince B.A. Golitsyn went to join him there. The following day Peter sent a letter to Sophia demanding an explanation for the apparent mobilization of the musketeers, to which Sophia replied that she had merely summoned them as a bodyguard to accompany her on one of her customary monastery visits.[28] Even if this explanation were true, there can be little doubt that Sophia saw the musketeers as the last resort in contesting Peter's increasingly open challenge to her authority and there is every indication that she hoped for a repeat performance of 1682. But times had changed: the depleted Naryshkin faction could no longer convincingly be held up as a butt for musketeer fury, especially now that the tensions and ambiguities of the succession crisis were absent; the musketeers themselves were less disturbed and sensitive that they had been at the time of Tsar Fedor's death; and, perhaps more important, Peter's party now had the tsar himself as its spokesman. Even though Peter was clearly not the sole instigator of the current break with Sophia, he was more than willing to listen to evidence of her treachery, especially now that his own life seemed threatened. A series of strongly worded directives in Peter's name were sent from the Trinity Monastery to the musketeers and soldiers regiments ordering them to join their rightful sovereign. The first of these, which arrived in Moscow on August 16, was ignored by the troops in the belief that it was counterfeit and Sophia was for a while successful in preventing the musketeers from deserting the capital in response to Peter's summons. Golitsyn himself received one of Peter's rescripts, as did foreign officers still stationed in the capital, but Gordon was ordered by the prince to ignore the summons.[29]

Shortly after this the patriarch added his weight to Peter's cause by leaving Moscow for the Trinity Monastery, and on August 27 Peter's summons was repeated, this time with better results, for rumors that the documents were "counterfeit" were wearing thin. In an attempt to resolve the crisis and maybe to discuss terms with her brother, Sophia herself set out for the monastery accompanied by a large retinue on August 29, but was ordered to turn back.[30] Golitsyn, it is said, at this point retired to his estate at Medvedkovo, a not uncharacteristic gesture in a situation which must have been increasingly distressing.

The most open challenge so far came on September 1, when a unit of musketeers loyal to Peter arrived in

the capital to demand the handover of Shaklovity, Silvester Medvedev and other members of Sophia's party.[31]
Sophia refused and, playing for time, tried out the old
ploy of hinting at imminent danger to Tsar Ivan. According to Gordon she delivered a long eloquent speech
in which she listed the achievements of her administration, reminded the musketeers of her good will towards
them and concluded: "It is not Fedor Shaklovity's head
they seek but mine, and that of Tsar Ivan Alekseevich."[32] Brandy was distributed to the troops and, according to Gordon, Sophia delivered a similar speech to
merchants, townspeople and others gathered in the Kremlin.

On September 3 we have the first clear evidence
(again from Gordon) of positive action on Golitsyn's
part. He sent a messenger to his cousin Boris Alekseevich asking him to act as an instrument to unite the
parties. Boris advised him to hasten to the monastery
and appeal for the tsar's favor.[33] If Gordon's evidence
is correct, it indicates that Golitsyn was now isolated
and no longer a party to the schemes of Sophia and
Shaklovity. Solov'ev, for one, is convinced that the
prince "took no part in the activities in Moscow."[34]

The next day foreign military personnel received a
letter from Peter commanding them to join him. Gordon
showed this letter to Golitsyn, who appeared perturbed
by it and undecided as to the best course of action. He
promised to advise Gordon before nightfall after he had
showed the letter to Sophia and Tsar Ivan, but the
foreigners decided not to wait.[35] By now the time had
turned against Sophia; on September 6 musketeer representatives, increasingly aware of where the real power
lay, told her to give up Skaklovity, whom they would
accompany to the Trinity Monastery. Like Tsaritsa Natalia, who had unsuccessfully shielded her brother Ivan
in 1682, Sophia was forced to comply.[36] When Golitsyn
heard the news of Shaklovity's arrest he was "much
moved and consternated." Most of the boyars who had
remained in town now set off to join Peter, and Golitsyn, who spent the night of September 6-7 on his estate
at Medvedkovo, decided to follow them. He arrived at
the gates of the Trinity Monastery in the afternoon of
the 7th with a group of close associates, including
Leonty Nepliuev, Venedikt Zmeev, Grigory Kosogov and
Emel'ian Ukraintsev, but the party was not admitted to
the monastery compound.[37] Gordon spoke to the prince
that night and found him "somewhat melancholious, for
which he had good cause."[38] That same day Shaklovity
had been arrested, brought to the monastery and interrogated under torture, but had denied any complicity in
a plot on Peter's life or knowledge of Sophia's plans
to be crowned. The only thing he admitted was that an

attempt to "remove" Tsaritsa Natalia had been mooted. Golitsyn was spared interrogation, in fact he was denied any trial at all, and on September 9 he and his son were admitted to the monastery, where the following sentence was pronounced:

"Prince Vasily and Prince Aleksei Golitsyn! The great sovereign tsars and grand princes Ivan Alekseevich and Peter Alekseevich, autocrats of all the Great and Little and White Russias, order that it be made known to you: that they, the great sovereigns, deigned to occupy the throne of their ancestors and their sister...the great sovereign lady and noble princess and grand duchess Sophia Alekseevna, without their, the great sovereigns', counsel, did assume full autocratic power, and you, Prince Vasily and Prince Aleksei, abandoning them, the great sovereigns, and showing preference and favor to their royal sister, did report all manner of affairs to their sister, bypassing them, the great sovereigns; and they, the great sovereigns, were left in ignorance. And you, Prince Vasily, sent their, the great sovereigns', rescripts to the towns of Little Russia and ordered books to be printed with the name of their sister, the great sovereign lady and noble princess, without their, the great sovereigns', orders. And you, Prince Vasily, in this past year of 7197 (1689) were sent with the great sovereigns' men-at-arms into the Crimea and, reaching Perekop, you failed to carry out military operations and withdrew from that place and by this your lack of zeal great losses were inflicted on the royal treasury, ruin on the state and oppression on the people. For this the great sovereigns command that you be stripped of the rank of boyar, and your hereditary and service estates shall be transferred to the great sovereigns and shall be sent into exile to Kargopol'; and Fedor Martem'ianovich Bredikha shall be appointed your warder."[39]

Gordon records that Golitsyn had prepared a list of "services rendered" during his premiership, but was prevented from reading it out. It eventually reached the tsar, but made no impact upon him.[40] In De la Neuville's version, "the unfortunate prince, having made a bow and replying simply that it was difficult to justify himself before his master, withdrew."

Serious though the charges against Golitsyn were, they contained no reference to regicide or designs upon the crown. According to Gordon, the prince had his cousin Boris to thank for these omissions. Wishing to salvage the family honor, Boris Alekseevich had personally supervised the writing of Shaklovity's confession and taken the papers away, presumably to edit out anything that implicated Vasily Vasil'evich in treasonable acts.[42] Gordon comments that Golitsyn was "very well

known to be conscious if not a contriver of all intended against the lyfe of the youngest tzaar." On September 11 Shaklovity and the musketeer officers Kuz'ma
Chermny and Abrosim Petrov were executed.

Detailed arrangements were made for the dispatch
of Golitsyn and his family to Kargopol', a commercial
town on the River Onega, some 600 km to the north of
Moscow. Prince Vasily and Prince Aleksei were accompanied by their wives and younger children and a large
retinue of servants. Their warder Bredikha was instructed to keep a close watch over them, to intercept
"secret" letters and to prevent them submitting petitions to the crown. A unit of musketeers was assigned
to accompany them.[43] Meanwhile letters were sent to the
governor of Kargopol' with orders to make ready accommodation. Nothing was left to chance. The authorities
in Yaroslavl', one of the towns on the party's route,
was alerted to have ready a clerk and writing materials
so that Bredikha could report back to Moscow.[44] On September 14 Bredikha did forward a petition from the
Golitsyn: "Your slaves, Vas'ka and Aleshka" appealed to
the tsars in self-abasing terms, complaining about the
confiscation of their "wretched" estates, "falling
before the tsars' illustrious feet" and declaring their
loyalty. "We have served you, great sovereigns, with
devoted service and good will, both as military commanders and in ambassadorial affairs, and have always
carried out your great sovereigns' commands with the
greatest of zeal, as though they were God's." They
begged to be allowed to withdraw to their estates in
Rostov and Yaroslavl'. Another petition requested that
most of their servants be returned to Moscow as they
had not the means to support them.[45] On September 15
the exiles were transferred to a new warder, Pavel
Mikhailovich Skriabin, who was to remain with them
until 1692. Their retinue was reduced to 25 and Skriabin was ordered to make an inventory of their possessions, allowing them to retain goods to the value of
2,000 rubles and their wives' carriages. There appeared
now to be some confusion about the party's destination,
possibly because some of Golitsyn's enemies considered
Kargopol' insufficiently severe. In a memorandum to
Skriabin of September 15 the penal colony at Pustozersk
was mentioned, but on September 18 the destination was
changed to Yarensk, several hundred kilometers further
east than Kargopol'.[46] In Yaroslavl' on September 23
the Golitsyns were for the first time questioned about
their part in the "musketeer plots", threats to the
lives of Peter and Tsaritsa Natalia, a plan to burn
down the palace at Preobrazhenskoe and Sophia's misuse
of the royal titles and desire to be crowned. Both
swore that they had no knowledge of any of Shaklovity's

plans and Prince Vasily wrote, in a petition, that he
swore "before God himself in his heaven, before his
redeeming throne, that Fedka Shaklovity was never a
close friend of mine, Vas'ka's, but that we were simply
acquaintances." He referred to the service record of
his family, "who had always served the tsars' ancestors
faithfully, not begrudging their lives, dying for the
royal honor and taking part in no wicked deed."[47] This
petition, like most of those which followed it, had no
effect. The government took pains to root out evidence
to prove the close friendship between Golitsyn and
Shaklovity, citing in particular dispatches from the
Crimean campaigns.

The party made its way slowly north-eastwards,
passing through Vologda in early October, Tot'ma at the
beginning of November, Sol'vychegodsk in December and
reaching Yarensk on January 5, 1690.[48] At Vologda a
messenger had arrived from Sophia, with a letter of
condolence and a sum of money, but the tsarevna's influence could be of little use now that she herself was
under arrest and confined in the Novodevichy Convent.[49]
Just before they reached Tot'ma they suffered an acci-
dent, which Golitsyn recounted in a petition: "We suffer, poor things, and are close to death, but we have
been falsely accused. When they brought us, your
slaves, to Tot'ma, before we reached the town, on the
River Sukhon, the carriages bearing our wives and
children and serving people fell into the water and our
wives and small children were dragged with difficulty
from the river and lay unconscious for a long time."[50]
At Tot'ma Aleksei's wife gave birth, probably prema-
turely, to twin girls who died shortly afterwards.[51]

Yarensk proved to be a dismal spot. Even the
gaoler Skriabin, who was forever complaining about his
duties and asking to be relieved of them, reported that
it was "a most wretched town; in all, with crown assistants, clerks and the guard, there are 30 households.
The people of the district rarely visit the town; they
decide matters amongst themselves and collect the
tsars' taxes amongst themselves. We have all the heart-
ache!"[52] His captives were equally unimpressed. "And
we, poor innocent people, and our small worms of children have nothing and we are held in captivity, in poor
conditions and in despair of our lives. We shall die a
hungry and painful death." They found Yarensk, where
they were confined in a two-roomed wooden house, "a
place most wretched, poor and unpopulated, with all
manner of hardships which even the local people are
unable to endure."[53] Numerous petitions were sent off
to Moscow. On March 7, 1690: "We are in the most dire
need, not only of clothing but also of food."[54] On
March 16 they begged Tsar Ivan to lead them "from death

to life, from darkness to light."[55] A petition of August 10 contained a somewhat pathetic reference to the birth of yet another daughter to Tsar Ivan's wife, in the hope that the joyous event might be the occasion for mercy.[56] The pleas of poverty and "closeness to death" were probably exaggerated. An inventory taken by Skriabin in Yarensk showed that the family still possessed a number of robes, silver plates and cutlery, icons, clocks and books,[57] but the lack of variety in local food supplies and the simplicity of their accommodation must have been something of a shock for people who had been amongst the richest in Moscow. On October 23, 1690 a rescript from Moscow gave permission to the family servants to return to the capital, but most chose to remain.[58]

On March 7, 1691, as a result of the investigation of Silvester Medvedev (executed in February 1691) a decree was issued for the removal of the Golitsyns to Pustozersk. They were to be given a daily allowance of 13 altyn 2 denga.[59] At least one set of new allegations against Golitsyn was discredited. A monk by the name of Iosif testified that he had been in Yarensk and heard various confessions from the prince, including a hint that Peter had only a year to live. Later it was found that Iosif had fabricated the whole story and had never been anywhere near Yarensk, but the opportunity was taken in the meantime to subject Golitsyn to all the old questions about his participation in the "plots" of 1689.[60] The most fanciful new accusations came from the Pole Mitka Silin, who had lived in Medvedev's house. Medvedev, he claimed, had asked him to prophesy (Silin claimed the gift of second sight) whether Golitsyn would be tsar, Shaklovity "first prince" and Medvedev patriarch. Apparently Golitsyn and Medvedev told Silin of their plot to kill Peter, his mother and other Naryshkins and to exile the patriarch. Sophia and Golitsyn were to marry. Silin, however, said that he saw bad omens for such a scheme. On another occasion Golitsyn is said to have summoned him and asked him to look into the future, but accused the Pole of being mad when he predicted a bad outcome.[61] Golitsyn, of course, denied all the Pole's accusations, but denials were brushed aside and the family was moved on.

The prospect of Pustozersk was not a pleasant one. The colony was located on the White Sea at the mouth of the River Pechora and had already accommodated a number of eminent exiles, including Artamon Matveev and Archpriest Avvakum. By March 31 the party was in Sol'vychegodsk, from where Skriabin wrote to complain that there were no boats available to transport them further and asked for clearer instructions.[62] On April 4 the Golitsyns sent a conventional petition to the tsars, with reference to their children aged five (Mikhail Alekseevich), two (Mikhail Vasil'evich), and a new-born baby of five weeks, no doubt in the hope of tugging at the royal heartstrings.[63] No rescript of mercy arrived from Moscow and by the beginning of July they had reached the mouth of the River Dvina, where a band of musketeers joined them. On July 1, as the prospect of Pustozersk loomed larger, Golitsyn wrote: "In Pustozersk bread is very expensive as is every kind of sustenance, and we, your slaves, shall die a hungry and painful death."[64] The colony's remoteness is indicated by an enquiry sent from the Chancellery of Criminal Investigation to the Razriad (July 14, 1691) asking the name of the current governor of Pustozersk. Meanwhile Skriabin's pleas were finally heeded and he was granted leave to return to Moscow once he had delivered his charges to governor I.M. Leont'ev in Pustozersk.[65]

Skriabin was never to complete this particular mission. On July 1 attempts to set sail for Pustozersk from Archangel had been foiled by the weather. Even Eng[lish ships], writes Skria[b]in, were anchored at the mou[th of the Dvina afraid to] set sail.[66] After another att[empt they docked at the R]iver Mezen', from where the Gol[itsyns sent yet another] petitions from "your poor and help[less slaves Vas'ka] and Aleshka Golitsyn, who hav[e no ... anywhere sav]e God alone." They described [the terrible storm that] had almost cost them their liv[es, and a second time w]hen they had almost been shi[pwrecked. "And because] of that storm we, your sla[ves, and our wives and ch]ildren were terribly sick, and [especially the small chi]ldren, and we suffered from swe[lling and ...ness a]nd we lie in this place dreadfully sick and do not expect to survive." They begged to be spared the journey mentioning that many craft had been lost on the way to Pustozersk.[67]

The party was now at least three weeks' journey from its destination overland, a route which could be traversed only by reindeer sleighs, with no sheltering places on the way. They must, therefore, have been relieved to receive a royal decree, issued in November, allowing them to stay in Mezen' until the spring. This was only a temporary stay of execution, and in February 1692 when their removal again seemed imminent the Golitsyns sent a long petition to the crown containing all imaginable pleas, including references to the tender ages of their children, protests at the cruelty of sending women and children across the seas, complaints about the inadequacy of their allowance and appeals to the names of the saints and the tsar's daughters. They ended: "Gracious great sovereign tsars and grand princes Ioann Alekseevich and Peter Alekseevich, autocrats of all the Great and White and Little Russias, pity us, your slaves, poor and destitute and tormented, regard us with favor and do not send us to Pustozersk, but allow us to be receive back in Moscow."68

This appeal must have had some effect for in April a decree extended their stay in Mezen'. "April 1 (1692) the great sovereign tsars... do grant Prince Vasily and his son Prince Aleksei Golitsyn that they shall not be sent to the settlement of Pustozersk but shall remain in Kevrol' until the great sovereigns decree otherwise, and the governor of Kevrol' and Mezen' shall take charge of them and they shall receive the same allowance as previously from the great sovereigns from the local customs and tavern revenues in Kevrol' and Mezen'."69 Skriabin was finally allowed to return to Moscow, and in June the prisoners were handed over to governor Khomutov of Mezen'. From this date evidence of petitions is scantier. Despite the postponement of removal to Pustozersk, life on Mezen' was no treat. In a petition of February 1693, in which Golitsyn also referred to the birth of Tsar Ivan's daughter Anna, the future empress, he writes: "We are dying a painful and tormenting death, and are suffering terribly from lack of food and clothing, for no grain is sown in Mezen' but it is imported at a high price."70 In March after many appeals for permission to send aid to the exiles, Golitsyn's mother-in-law Nastas'ia Ivanovna Streshneva was allowed to send a number of small items and 80 rubles in cash. The gifts included a number of lengths of cloth (fine and coarse linen, canvas etc.), 4 men's shirts, 4 children's blouses, 4 female headdresses (kokoshniki and podubrusniki), 10 towels, 2 reels of thread, 2 pairs of children's boots and stockings, a woman's blouse, child's kaftan and 2 pairs of scissors.71 These were received in April.

One of the last surviving petitions from the Golitsyns (April 8, 1693) was intended for delivery to Peter when he made a projected visit to the north of Russia, but it was sent direct to Moscow like all the rest. "We beg, falling and laying our heads and our little children beneath your royal and illustrious feet, kissing them and covering them with our tears -- be merciful, be merciful to us destitute and tormented orphans."72 If Peter saw this document he was no more inclined to mercy than on other occasions. In February 1694 a new governor was appointed in Mezen'. The last direct reference to the prisoners in Mezen' is contained in a letter from the retiring governor Khomutov, dated February 27, as a covering note to yet another petition. The petition breaks off after the first few conventional lines.73

Evidence has yet to come to light of the subsequent fate of the Golitsyns. It is not known whether

they were sent to Pustozersk, for the next news of the
family finds them in Pinega (formerly Volokopinezhskaia
volost') in Archangel province. In April 1713 provin-
cial governors were ordered to send details of allowances being paid to non-servitors and in one reply,
from A.A. Kurbatov, vice-governor of Archangel, dated
May 20 1714, it is recorded that since 1709 the Golitsyn family had been allocated one ruble per day. There
had been some plan to transfer Golitsyn yet again, but
he had died on April 21, 1714.[74] This date is confirmed
by the inscription on the prince's tombstone in the
grounds of the Krasnogorsko-Bogoroditsky Monastery outside Pinega, which was transcribed by one E.S. in 1886:
"Beneath this stone lie the remains of the boyar Prince
Vasil'evich Golitsyn, deceased on the 21st of April in
the 69th (?) year of his life."[75] According to E.S.
there had been an improvement in the Golitsyns' circumstances. In 1711 the family owned two houses, one in
Pinega itself, the other some 20 versts away, and
Golitsyn was even able to make a few bequests to the
Krasnogorsky Monastery, where he spent many hours in
the last years of his life. E.S. mentions a copy of the
Prologue, inscribed by Golitsyn, two embroidered silk
icons of the Virgin and the Crucifixion, a shroud
depicting the Deposition from the Cross and an old
gilded mirror -- the latter a poignant reminder, perhaps, of more prosperous times.[76] At the end of his
short article E.S. appealed to Golitsyn's descendants
to erect a memorial over his simple grave, a suggestion
which was discussed in the same journal by family historian N.N. Golitsyn in December 1886. A subscription
fund was opened, but whether the project was ever completed is not known.[77]

There is a postscript to the story. On July 29
1714, in response to the news in Kurbatov's letter,
Golitsyn's wife and son Aleksei were released from exile.[78] Evdok'ia Ivanovna, who had suffered so many hardships as a result of her husband's disgrace, appears to
have lived on until at least 1724.[79] Aleksei, who at
the height of his father's career had himself enjoyed
rank and honors, including the deputy directorship of
the Foreign Office, had lost his wits (otupel) as a
result of his confinement. He lived on until 1740, a
half-mad recluse.[80] Prince Vasily's son Mikhail probably died in exile, but Mikhail Alekseevich, a child of
two when the family was banished, appears to have been
released before his grandfather's death. It is recorded
that he married for the first time in 1711, and later
earned notoriety at the court of Empress Anna as page
and court jester. He did a period of service in the
navy and in the 1720s converted temporarily to Catholicism. He died in 1775.[81] Had Prince Vasily, too, been

broken by his experiences? We still have no direct evidence of his state of mind after the last incomplete petition of 1694 and can only speculate on his thoughts and activities during the last twenty years of his life.

# CHAPTER SIX

## THE MAN AND HIS ERA

In verses to a portrait of Golitsyn engraved during Sophia's regency, the author, who may have been Silvester Medvedev or even the tsarevna herself, makes reference to the mounted warrior on the Golitsyn coat-of-arms. This device, the symbol of martial exploits, was "ofttimes crowned with glorious honor" but, the writer continues:

> Not you, but the image of the renowned prince,
> In all lands where it is inscribed,
> Henceforth shall shine forth with glory
> And glorify the name of Golitsyn everywhere.[1]

In other words, the ancient heraldic device of the Grand Duchy of Lithuania, the birthplace of the Golitsyn clan, had been superceded by the image of Prince Vasily, whose feats of valor had made him worthy to become the symbol of his family. These sentiments were characteristic of the "official" image of Golitsyn fostered by Sophia, which in the end did scant justice to a man whose real qualities and achievements were sufficiently great to stand alone, unaided by exaggeration or distortion of the facts. After Sophia's downfall the image naturally suffered a reversal. A virtual silence fell over the "great" Golitsyn, who, if he was mentioned at all was denegrated for his connection with Sophia, who "threw the government into great convulsions" and "fill'd the State with continual plots and conspiracies."[2] For a long time it was impossible to consider Golitsyn in isolation from Sophia and the following extract from an early 18th-century history of Peter's reign provides a typical analysis:

"Golitsyn was the ablest Politician at the Time in Muscovy, the most learned and accomplished of all the Boyars; a Friend to Foreigners; and an Encourager of Industry; He would indeed have been without Exception, had not his Affection for his Mistress led him beyond the Bonds of his Duty, and involved him in the Ruin of that ambitious Woman. It was chiefly owing to his Advice and Dexterity, that she was able long to maintain her vast Authority; which she, in Return, exerted to the utmost for his Support, against those of the Boyars, who were in the Interest of the Czar Peter."[3]

Sophia's regency, of course, long remained in the shadow of that "greatest of great men" Peter, whose accomplishments were so much more dramatic. Nevertheless Sophia's administration did prompt some favorable comment even in the eighteenth century, for example from Catherine the Great who remarked that "we cannot but own, that she was very capable of governing",4 or from Prince B.I. Kurakin, who wrote: "The administration of Tsarevna Sophia Alekseevna was from the beginning most vigorous and just and pleasing to the people--never had there been such a wise administration in the Russian state. And in the period of her regency, in seven years, the state reached a pinnacle of prosperity."5

In general, however, the regency had to wait for later, less Peter-oriented times for a more enthusiastic assessment. C.B. O'Brien, for example, thought it "a government of unusual distinction and promise, which pursued with intelligence and imagination the interests of Russia abroad and introduced reforms at home that are generally believed to have originated in succeeding generations"6 The extent of the disagreement may be gauged by comparing the above with the following passage from N. Ustrialov's official history of Peter's reign:  "In the acts issued in the seven years of her administration we find nothing remarkable either for the good of society or for the development of the nations's industrial strength or for its education, nothing to compare with those statutes which distinguished the reigns of Aleksei Mikhailovich and Fedor Alekseevish, not to mention the fact that there is not a trace of Peter's far-sighted wisdom."7

Golitsyn's own achievements are not, of course, synonymous with the overall record of Sophia's regency, especially if we accept that he was a man of vision, as remarkable for ideas as for concrete accomplishments. Equally, it is difficult to estimate the prince's personal contribution to "progressive" measures orginating in chancelleries not subject to his direct supervision, for example the lightening of penalties for certain crimes, decrees on the maintenance of public order and the establishment of the Slavonic-Greek-Latin Academy. His own political accomplishments fell primarily within the sphere of the Foreign Office and include not only well publicized successes like the treaty of "permanent peace" with Poland in 1686 but also lesser known activities such as the encouragement of foreign manufacturers and the supervision of architectural projects. Equally important were his services in improving Russia's image abroad by both public and private contacts with foreigners, diplomatic correspondence and the dispatch of numerous delegations. Golitsyn appeared as an unusually good ambassador for a country which many foreigners deemed capable of producing only "savages", and it is foreigners -- Patrick Gordon, Franz Lefort, Philippe Avril, De la Neuville, Laurent Rinhuber and others -- to whom we must turn for our most detailed portraits of the prince. As Georg Schleissing wrote:

"He was a great lover of all manner of knowledge and learning, which makes him a very strange beast indeed in Russia."[8] To quote from De la Neuville: "This Prince Golitsyn is without doubt one of the most intelligent, the most refined and most magnificent men that this country, which he intended to place on a par with others, has ever produced. He spoke Latin well and was overjoyed to meet foreigners."[9]

The prince's knowledge of foreign languages, an unusual talent amongst Russians of his generation, was just one of the gifts that foreigners remarked upon. Schleissing, for example, records that "he made himself fluent in foreign languages, especially Latin, in which he was so accomplished that he had not only a fine style of writing but also commanded an elegant skill in Latin conversation."[10] Other writers suggest that he also knew some Greek, Polish and German,[11] but our sources do not reveal where or when Golitsyn acquired his knowledge. Recognition of the prince's linguistic gifts is obliquely indicated in a curious letter written from Hamburg in 1686 by Heinrich Kellerman, the son of one of Moscow's leading foreign merchants. Kellerman, who had spent several years studying in the West, wrote to the prince offering to correct the Slavonic text of the Bible and appending examples in a variety of languages of discrepancies in the translation of the scriptures. Unseemly though it was for a non-Orthodox foreigner to make such a proposal to a secular official, Golitsyn invited Kellerman to return to Russia, but his project was not carried out.[12]

Further evidence of Golitsyn's knowledge of languages and wide-ranging interests is provided by his book collection, which was catalogued along with other property after the confiscation of his estates. 93 books were discovered in his Moscow mansion, whilst others found in houses and churches on other estates brought the total up to 216, both printed and in manuscript. The perfunctory descriptions given by the cataloguing clerks rarely allow precise identification of authors and titles, or even of the language used. Direct mention is made of 7 books in German, 2 in Polish and a Polish-Latin grammar. Secular literature predominated and included works on history (e.g. a history in Polish, a copy of the Kiev chronicle), military affairs (a book on the art of warfare published in Moscow in 1649, the "military statute of the Dutch State"), "an illustrated book on fishes and beasts", a book on land surveying in German, a manuscript copy of Yury Krizhanich, Hiob Ludolf's History of Abyssinia (probably the one presented by Laurent Rinhuber in 1684), a medical primer for the treatment of horses, a book on diplomatic protocol, translations of Polish

tales and a number of grammars and calendars. Amongst
the religious books, alongside the standard service and
prayer books, lives of saints and writings of the
Church fathers, were works by contemporary Russian
clerics such as Simeon Polotsky, Dmitry Rostovsky and
Lazar Baranovich.[13] In addition to his own thematically
rather haphazard collection, Golitsyn also had access
to the library of the Foreign Office which by the 1680s
had amassed a sizeable collection of works, all in the
foreign languages, for the use of its staff. Latin,
which Golitsyn read fluently, was the predominant language. By 1696 there were over 333 books in the library, including histories, atlases, topographies, law
codes and statutes, grammars and lexicons, Protestant
and Catholic religious treatises.[14] On at least one
occasion Golitsyn is recorded as having borrowed a collection of architectural manuals from the library.

One should not exaggerate Golitsyn's sophistication in matters of learning. His library, for example,
may have been unusually comprehensive by the standards
of Muscovy in the 1680s, but was meager in comparison
with the collections of some contemporary Western aristocrats, politicians and scholars. One will recall,
also, that Golitsyn still adhered in part to the Muscovite style of diplomatic negotiations in which great
store was set by the correct formulation of royal titles and other minutiae of diplomatic protocol. Some of
the questions which he is recorded as having put to
foreigners appear naive and reveal considerable gaps in
his knowledge of European affairs. In particular,
Golitsyn has been accused of failing to shake off "ves-
tiges of antiquity". Despite his education he was "unable to free himself from the superstitiousness of his
age."[15] During the investigations that took place after
his exile, for example, Golitsyn was accused of enga-
ging in black magic and consulting soothsayers, and is
said to have kept a peasant "sorcerer" in his bathhouse
who prepared drugged food and potions for Sophia to
maintain her love for him.[16] Golitsyn denied these and
other allegations, which may easily be dismissed as the
conventional ingredients of trumped-up charges in a
superstitious age, but other incidents have more of a
ring of truth about them. One story, reported by
Zheliabuzhsky and subsequent writers, tells how in 1689
one Ivan Bundakov was observed to pick up some earth
from Golitsyn's footprint and was tortured at the
prince's request as it was believed that preserving
earth from a print could bring about the victim's illness or death. Bundakov explained that he suffered from
falling sickness and took earth from the places where
his attacks occurred.[17] Another incident, in 1687, when
Golitsyn reprimanded officers for appearing on parade

dressed in black may have stemmed from his anxiety
about the effect of such a display upon the rank-and-
file as much as from his own superstitiousness. The
case of the trial and execution of the Silesian Protestant mystic Quirinus Kuhlmann must be dismissed as
evidence of Golitsyn's superstitiousness and intoler-
ance for the prince was away in the Crimea when Kuhlmann arrived and was interrogated, and exiled before
the execution was carried out.[18]

The case for Golitsyn's superstitiousness as a
counterbalance to his tolerant open-mindedness is a
weak one, especially when one bears in mind his willingness to consult foreign doctors (Von Gaden before
1682, Rinhuber in 1684) and his free contacts with
foreigners in a period when "heretics" were still believed to contaminate those Russians with whom they
came into contact. Golitsyn even visited homes in Moscow's foreign colony and is credited with a program of
free entry for foreigners to Russia and incentives to
Russians to travel abroad. De la Neuville writes: "He
permitted (the nobles) to send their children to Latin
colleges in Poland, advising them to summon Polish tutors for the others, and accorded to foreigners access
to and exit from the kingdom, which had never been
practised before him. He also wished the nobility to
travel out of the country and to learn how to make war
in foreign countries."[19] De la Neuville exaggerates the
novelty of Golitsyn's program. Foreign personnel had
been entering Russia in large numbers since the 1620s,
whilst the practice of sending nobles abroad to study,
except for a small-scale experiment under Boris Godu-
nov, was initiated by Peter I. There is no evidence
that Golitsyn had a clear-cut "program" on these matters, but his own behavior and comments may have convinced De la Neuville that such a program existed.

Another of Golitsyn's attitudes that distanced him
even further from the traditionally conservative and
insular Muscovite nobility was his sympathy towards
Catholics. For both historical and theological reasons
the Russian Orthodox Church had always been more wary
of the Church at Rome than of the various Protestant
sects and by the 1680s Catholics had still not been
granted permission to build a church in the Foreign
Colony, whilst Protestants had four. Moscow's small
Catholic community and their friends abroad must therefore have been overjoyed when Golitsyn emerged as their
"patron". There were many signs of his sympathy, for
example the comparative ease with which a Jesuit chap-
laincy was established in 1684, the prince's friendship
with Patrick Gordon, his friendly reception of Marizio
Vota, Georgius David and Avril and Beauvollier. Father
Schmidt, the first Jesuit chaplain in Moscow, who left

in 1688, wrote to Golitsyn from Smolensk thanking him for the fact that his stay in Moscow had been ameliorated "by Your Grace's extensive concern for the spiritual comfort of the Catholics."[20] As recorded previously Golitsyn was not able entirely to ignore the disapproval of the Church, especially of the xenophobic Patriarch Joachim, but still the authorities deemed it wise to wait for the prince's downfall before expelling the Jesuits. A decree of October 1689 alleged that the Jesuits were "the cause of much harm to the Holy Apostolic Church with their printed sheets and images on canvas, bone and other artful devices; and there is much dissension between the Holy Apostolic Eastern Church and the Western Church at Rome." It was stressed that the mission had only been allowed temporarily, "for brotherly friendship and love toward His Majesty the Emperor of Rome."[21]

David, one of the expelled priests, was in no doubt that Golitsyn's downfall was to blame for their dismissal: "The reason for our expulsion was the Prince Golitsyn's good will towards us and now his exile; the overthrow of the Tsarevna Sophia who, when she learned of our expulsion lamented greatly; the hatred of the patriarch and the clergy, with whom we have never been on good terms... But we rejoice that we have been deemed worthy to suffer insult in the name of Jesus."[22] Elsewhere he referred to Golitsyn as "most renowned for his kindness towards foreigners and for his dexterity in affairs of state."[23] He also provided some interesting theories about the strength of the prince's sympathies. He suggests, for example, that Tsar Fedor wished to invite Jesuits to teach in Moscow and that Sophia, with Golitsyn's support, had intended to institute this scheme, despite the opposition it was bound to provoke from the Orthodox authorities.[24]

Golitsyn's "flirtation" with Catholicism was almost certainly prompted by political rather than theological considerations. He did not participate actively in the doctrinal dispute which raged in the 1680s between "Graecophiles" and "Latinizers", even though his political sympathies must have been on the side of the latter, who adhered to Sophia's camp. Nor is there any evidence that he was a convert; on the contrary, available evidence points to the fact that he carried out his religious duties strictly and conscientiously -- attending the vigil at Tsar Fedor's tomb in 1682, parading with icons and crosses before the Crimean campaigns, making pilgrimages to monasteries and churches. Like many well-off Muscovite nobles, he had churches built on his estates and he bequeathed gifts to monasteries and churches. He owned religious books and icons. In addition he personally supervised investigations of Old Believer activities and attended torture sessions. There is even a hint that he found consolation in religion at the end of his life, although, as his grave stone confirms, he did not take monastic vows. On the other hand, none of these activities testify to an excess of religious zeal. In an age and society where failure to observe certain rites and ceremonies could result in charges of heresy, it is difficult to reach any firm conclusions about the intensity of Golitsyn's faith.

Foreigners often described Golitsyn as "humane" or "kind" and subsequent historians have made him out to be something of a social reformer with, amongst other things, a scheme for the abolition of serfdom to his credit. O'Brien, for example, claimed that Golitsyn had "explored the problem of the emancipation of the serfs."[25] This was endorsed by the pre-revolutionary social historian Semevsky, chiefly on the grounds that such a scheme was fully in keeping with the known facts of Golitsyn's character and inclinations.[26] The only contemporary witness, however, for the existence of such a plan is De la Neuville, who tells us that Golitsyn "gathered information about the condition of European states and their governments and wished to begin with the emancipation of the peasants, to provide them with land, which they now cultivate for the profit of the tsar, and have them pay a yearly tax instead." Such a scheme, it was calculated, would double current revenue.[27] Unfortunately no information is yet to hand to corroborate this statement. If Golitsyn really intended to free the serfs and to supply them with land, he was far ahead of his time and his downfall becomes a double tragedy. We cannot rule out the possibility that he cherished long-term hopes for such a radical measure, but no abolitionist sympathies are reflected in the legislation of Sophia's regency.[28] On the contrary, the measures enacted were, broadly speaking, aimed at keeping the serfs firmly attached to their masters's estates, in adherence to the Code of Laws of 1649. They included decrees to restore to their owners peasants who fled during the troubles of 1682,[29] reiteration of penalties for harboring fugitives[30] and numerous piecemeal attempts to settle misunderstandings and inconsistencies in the laws governing land tenure, the inheritance of estates etc.[31] When deviations from this pattern occurred they met the interests of other sections of the population useful to the crown, e.g. the decrees of 1684 and 1685 allowing runaway peasants who had succeeded in being registered as townspeople (posadskie liudi) to retain their urban status in order not to unbalance the collective tax-paying obligations of the townpeople.[32] There is no direct evidence that

91

Golitsyn initiated these and similar measures, but it must be said that if he did favor emancipation, he did not apply the ideal in his personal affairs. At the time of his exile when all his property was inspected and valued prior to transfer to the crown or new owners, he had as many as 50 estates in 20 different regions.[33] Only three of these had been inherited from his father. The rest were acquired through marriage, by purchase and, the majority, by royal endowment in recognition of services rendered in the Ukraine, the Foreign Office, the Crimean Campaigns and for other exploits. These estates, which yielded considerable revenues, were run on conventional lines using peasant labor to provide corvée or quitrent, according to local conditions. On three of the estates potash deposits were mined by serf labor, whilst Golitsyn employed as many as 400 slaves in his Moscow household. He was one of the wealthiest landowners of his day, a direct beneficiary of the Muscovite feudal order. He was fully capable of championing causes detrimental to his own class, as the abolition of the Code of Precedence illustrates, but there are no signs that he moved towards the even more radical step of abolishing peasant bondage in his own estates.

Although De la Neuville's list of Golitsyn's schemes included a number of less ambitious, more practical ventures, such as improvement of road and river transport, development of the Siberian fur trade and trade routes with China,[34] his grandiose but unfulfilled plan to emancipate the serfs and his even more Utopian desire to "colonise deserts, enrich beggars, transform savages into men, cowards into heroes and herdsmen's huts into stone palaces"[35] has earned him the reputation of being a "dreamer". A. Tereshchenko, the author of a somewhat unreliable biographical essay, writes that Golitsyn, "seduced by the future of his reveries, abandoned himself to the rash impulses of his passions. He pictured his alluring, brilliance beyond in the bright colors of the imagination."[36] This assessment takes little account of the complex and arduous duties which Golitsyn was called upon to perform. He may have had visions of a better Russia, but he scarcely had time to remain a passive dreamer. He proved himself to be capable of determined action in both administration and diplomacy, and any shortcomings in his record must, in the long run, be blamed on the failure of the 17th-century Russian government to "divide the labors" of its officials or to make any clear distinction between civil and military posts. Thus Golitsyn, whose talents were best suited to the Foreign Office, was also required to serve as commander-in-chief of the army and dissipate his energies in the fruitless Crimean campaigns. His earlier period of service in the Ukraine also kept him away from the government chancelleries where his talents might have been better employed. Golitsyn was one of the many wasted lives in Russian history, prevented by stagnant traditions from realising his full potential.

Another of Golitsyn's activities which is worthy of attention is his patronage of architecture. De la Neuville lists amongst his public building projects the first stone bridge over the Moskva river,[37] new premises for the Foreign Office and "more than 3,000 stone houses."[38] The latter may refer to a law of October 1688 which urged nobles to build their town houses of stone with nonflammable roof coverings.[39] Many public and royal works were supervised by the Foreign Office and in some cases carried out by the chancellery's team of architects and craftsmen. These included renovations to the Palace of Facets in the Kremlin, the decoration of the Foreign Office itself, additions and murals in the Kremlin towers and a number of churches and domestic buildings on palace estates and monasteries patronised by the royal family. In the 1680s architecture was perhaps more reflective than any other medium of Moscow's growing taste for Western styles. The newest style, later known as "Moscow Baroque", included decorative window surrounds, portals and pediments based on the Classical order system and showed a generally more symetrical approach to architectural design. The Foreign Office architects were responsible for some of the best examples of the style, such as the Church of Prince Josaphat (1688) on the royal estate at Izmailovo and external and internal decorations and fittings for the new buildings commissioned by Sophia in the Novedevichy Convent.[40]

One of the chief sources for the new designs were architectural manuals and other illustrated books of Western origin many of which found their way into Muscovite libraries, including the library of the Foreign Office. In the years 1684-85, for example, we learn that Golitsyn borrowed a number of books which had originally belonged to A.S. Matveev and "of those books... 17 with models of gardens, palaces and town-building, carving and fountains and sculptures, were taken from the Ambassadorial Chancellery by Prince Golitsyn to his home..."[41] It is not recorded what projects Golitsyn had in mind when he took these foreign books, but his own Moscow mansion and chapel and churches on his country estates were then in process of construction, as well as various state projects. On another occasion, in January 1685, Golitsyn ordered a Foreign Office clerk and artist to make a full description, measurements and a wooden model of the newly consecrated Cathedral of

93

the Resurrection in the monastery at New Jerusalem, commissioned by ex-Patriarch Nikon in the 1650s.[42] The cathedral was one of the most remarkable monuments of its era, exhibiting many novel features in both its exterior and interior design.

Golitsyn's interest in architectural fashion is exemplified by his mansion on Okhotny Riad in the center of Moscow. The exact starting date of construction is not known, but it will be recalled that fire destroyed a previous house in 1680. It was finished by 1689, with the exception of some of the outbuildings.[43] The house survived until the 1930s when it was demolished, despite the appeals of leading Soviet antiquarians. Surviving photographs show it to have been a two-storeyed building, its main facade capped by a simple triangular pediment (possibly a later addition) and decorated with window surrounds of typical Moscow Baroque design. A round archway led into an inner courtyard and the house was originally connected by a gallery to the adjoining Church of St. Paraskeva Piatnitsa, another Moscow Baroque building inspired by Ukrainian designs, which was singled out by Georgius David as one of the most elegant private chapels in Moscow.[44] The main living quarters consisted of 53 rooms and were adjoined by the usual servants' quarters, stables, store rooms, wine cellars etc.[45] De la Neuville was enthusiastic about the house, describing it as "one of the most magnificent in Europe; it is covered with copper, furnished with very rich tapestries and highly curious pictures."[46] The European analogy is almost certainly overdone. Golitsyn's house was remarkable for late 17th-century Moscow, where wood remained the standard building material for all but a privileged minority, but would have had thousands of rivals outside Russia. Nevertheless, it provides a fascinating glimpse at Golitsyn's tastes and lifestyle. The mansion and its contents were meticulously described, catalogued and valued in 1689-90 after it owner's exile.[47] From the documents we learn, for example, that the mansion contained 202 door and window apertures and that the metal-covered roof was laid by a Swedish craftsman called Gottfried Samoilov (Samuelson?) who has worked for the King of Sweden and was taken on by Golitsyn in August 1688.[48] The house was valued, without its roof, contents or land, at 12,883 rubles. With 1,700 for the roof, 1,040 for the land and a sum for fixtures and fitting (stoves, woodwork, windows etc.) government clerks estimated that the house was worth 16,154 rubles, 10 altyn and 4 denga.[49] This sum may be put into some kind of perspective by remembering that towards the end of their exile the Golitsyn family received a subsistence allowance of just 1 ruble per day.

The interior was fitted out with a fascinating mixture of traditional and foreign trappings. For example, in the main dining room, alongside the usual icons and frescoes depicting biblical scenes, hung portraits (persony) of Russian rulers (Vladimir the Great, Tsars Ivan IV, Fedor I, Mikhail, Aleksei, Fedor II, Peter and Ivan) and four "German prints". As in all the rooms, there were mirrors, and a German carved cabinet. The ceiling was decorated with a fresco depicting the sun, planets and signs of the zodiac, a subject which was in vogue in Moscow court circles.[50] The second dining room was adorned with a portrait of Golitsyn himself.[51] The centerpiece of the main bedroom was a German four-poster bed, lavishly carved with birds, plants and human faces. The occupants could look at both icons and five maps (zemlemernykh chertezhei).[52] The list of curiosities continues: the walls of one passageway were covered with red English cloth,[53] there were clocks (as many as 7 in one room), Indian and Persian carpets, German jugs, chests, stained glass, Venetian plates and dishes.[54] There were pictures and engravings everywhere. Prince Aleksei's room, for example, had pictures of the King and Queen of Poland, as well as twelve other framed portraits.[55] In an upper room there was yet another portrait of Tsar Fedor and one of Patriarch Nikon.[56] Even the outhouses were crammed with foreign items, presented to Golitsyn as gifts during his chancellorship or as the spoils of war. These included a collection of tents and "pavillions" (Turkish, Persian and Russian).[57] and Polish, Dutch and Austrian carriages.[58] A large gilded, painted, carved German carriage had glass windows and velvet upholstery.[59]

This rich array of possessions is indicative not only of Golitsyn's cosmopolitan tastes but also of his great wealth. He owned several other houses in the city and its environs, including his country estates at Chernaia Griaz', near the village of Bogoroditskoe, not far from Kolomenskoe, and Medvedkovo, to the north-east in the vicinity of Preobrazhenskoe.[60] Both of these estates had churches, built by their owner in 1684 and 1687 respectively, and their field, pastures, woodlands and fisheries supplied the boyar's household. His more remote estates, in the districts of Yaroslavl', Rostov, Suzdal' and other towns, were not used for private residence. In addition Golitsyn owned a wooden house on Smolensk Street, another on the Moskva River in the vicinity of the Novedevichy Convent and a small estate near the Foreign Colony on the Yauza River. The latter, which had a stone-built mansion, was purchased from a foreigner called David Bachart. After Golitsyn's exile it was transferred to the Pharmacy Chancellery, which used the grounds for growing medicinal herbs.[61]

The picture that emerges from this examination of Golitsyn's character and life-style tallies with the standard Soviet application of the term "transitional" to the era in which he lived. In some respects, such as adherence to the established Church, ownership of landed estates worked by serf labor and career pattern Golitsyn was a typical member of the Muscovite aristocracy. What distinguished him from most of his contemporaries was his receptiveness to the outside world -- his cultivation of foreign contacts, knowledge of their languages and countries, tolerance towards their religions. The architecture of his house was heavily influenced by Western European fashion, as were its contents. Had Golitsyn achieved a reconciliation with Peter in 1689 it is possible that he would have extended his knowledge by travelling abroad, but as it was this ardent Westerniser never went further than the Ukraine and spent the last 23 years of his life cut off from Western contacts. In the end it was the Muscovite system that destroyed him. Like many talented 18th-century Russians Golitsyn, despite his great gifts, relied on patronage for his elevation and once he reached the top was forced to apply himself to an impossibly large range of tasks. When he failed in the Crimea and his patroness fell from power mere talent was insufficient to save him.

# CONCLUSION

When Peter banished Golitsyn in September 1689 there is no doubt that he deprived himself of a potential adviser of great experience and ability, whose knowledge of Polish and Turkish affairs alone could have been put to good use in the tsar's subsequent foreign ventures, and whose open and inquisitive attitude towards foreigners and their customs was exactly that which Peter later fought hard to inculcate in many a reluctant noble. A. Brückner referred to him as a "spiritual relation" (Geistesverwandte) of Peter, despite the fact that they belonged to different parties.[1] It is hardly surprising, however, that in 1689 Peter failed to recognise these qualities, for the seventeen-year old should not be confused with the later emperor with his more cohesive view of Russia's role in European affairs. In 1689 Peter was in many way as still playing at politics, and manipulated by his mother's advisers, despite sporadic efforts to exert his authority. It was easy, for example, for his advisers to play upon the image of Golitsyn the defeated military commander and to gloss over his other achievements at a time when Peter was more interested in the art of warfare than in anything else. As Kliuchevsky remarked, Golitsyn was, in any case, more akin to the "liberal, somewhat meditative nobleman of Catherine's reign" and lacked those overtly practical, down-to-earth, even crude qualities favored by the young tsar in his henchmen.[2] Most important of all, Golitsyn was undeniably the closest aide of the sister whom Peter increasingly suspected of trying to usurp his power and perhaps even take his life. He remembered the massacres of 1682. Under these circumstances Golitsyn could not be saved, even though the evidence for his complicity in plots against Peter's life was flimsy.

Exile may have been inevitable in 1689, but why was no pardon ever forthcoming? Was it perhaps true that Peter "never forgave" his opponents? There is no evidence that Peter even contemplated allowing Golitsyn to return from exile and any thoughts in that direction would certainly have been overturned in 1698 when fresh disturbances amongst the musketeers renewed memories of Sophia's "plots" and rumors circulated that Golitsyn was to be recalled by Sophia and reinstated in power.[3] And so the prince remained in exile, almost forgotten by officialdom in the last years of his life, outliving Sophia by almost ten years. His fate was not, of course, unique. Many equally illustrious statesmen, before and after him, fell from favor, often as a result of factional struggles: A.S. Matveev and Alexander Menshikov are two of the most notable examples. That Golitsyn's image, albeit a distorted one, lived on in popular memory is illustrated by a cycle of historical songs (istoricheskie pesni) dating from the early 18th century and later.[4] In most of them Golitsyn returns from the wars, traversing difficult terrain and fearing disgrace in Moscow -- "Chto Moskvoiu kniaziu ekhat' - Moskvoi ochen' stydno". He bows before the tsar (or in one case Tsarevna Sophia)[5] and requests rewards, in some versions receiving a rebuff (derelict villages or even a noose), in others the town of Yaroslavl'. He makes another appearance in a light-hearted work published in Leipzig in 1737 in which he and General Hochmuth converse "in the realm of the dead."[6] The first substantial materials for an assessment of Golitsyn's career were published by N.I. Novikov in Drevniaia rossiiskaia vivliofika in 1791.[7] In the 19th century, with the "discovery" of pre-Petrine Russia, Golitsyn became a key figure in the process of preparation for the Tsar-Reformer. His significance for present-day historians remains much the same: a man of vision who remained too briefly in office to accomplish any of his more far-sighted schemes, an ardent adherent of the West who was ruined and banished by the greatest Westernizer of all.

_irony_

# APPENDIX I

## The Golitsyn Archive

One of the many developments of the Petrine age was the gradual emergence of the individual personality and its expression in personal writings. Peter epitomised the change: how shadowy many of his royal predecessors appear in comparison with the Great Tsar, who left not only the standard government decrees and gramoty but also numerous letters, diaries and other writings which, together with portraits done from life (a practice initiated only hesitantly in his father's reign) allow us to form a life-and-blood image. Peter outlived Golitsyn by only 11 years, but the latter belongs firmly to the Muscovite era in regard to the nature and quantity of the materials surviving for his biography. Like the vast majority of his contemporaries Golitsyn rarely expressed himself on paper in frank, personal terms, nor did he commit his private thoughts to diaries or autobiography. Even when he took up his pen for family correspondence the bulk of letters comprised conventional expressions of greeting and practical information. No personal letters from him to Sophia have come to light. Even the petitions written from exile, moving though they are, are written in the formal language of appeals to the crown.

The aim of this preamble is to suggest that even if a personal archive did exist, it would be unlikely to contain the sort of private writings one might expect from individuals born in Russia even a few decades later. As it is, there is no consolidated Golitsyn archive. Family historian N.N. Golitsyn writing in the 1890s, blamed the absence of a family archive comparable to those of the Vorontsovs of Sheremetevs on the lack of established seniority in the clan. Thus a unified collection of papers was not handed on.[1] In addition many losses and confiscations were suffered in the years 1725-42 when some members were in disgrace and, of course, Vasily Vasil'evich's property was confiscated in 1689.

Despite the consolidation and collection of papers which has taken place in Soviet times, the main catalogues of personal and family archives have no separate listing for V.V. Golitsyn.[2] The archive in TsGADA, f.1263, ed. khr. 11305, lists 50 Golitsyns, the eldest being Prince Vasily's cousing Mikhail Mikhailovich (1675-1730). A smaller collection in GIM, f.14, ed. khr. 4530 had papers dating from 1627, but again no direct reference to Vasily Vasil'evich. The lack of direct references does not, of course, rule out the possibility that materials may come to light, but the rumour recounted by a 19th-century historian that "in the archive of the College of Foreign Affairs there survive letters from Golitsyn to Sophia and from Sophia to Golitsyn, all his chancellery papers and plans for many undertakings" has not been corroborated in all details.[3] As was mentioned earlier, much of what we know about Golitsyn has to be acquired second-hand. Luckily what 17th-century Russians lacked in self-awareness, they made up for in a mania for detail. The obsession with inventories and valuations provides, quite inadvertantly, rich material for assessing Golitsyn's life-style, e.g. in the catalogues of his confiscated property. Finally, 17th-century visitors from the West were much less reticent than their Muscovite contemporaries and it is thanks to Golitsyn's love of foreigners that we know as much about him as we do.

# APPENDIX II

## Portraits of Golitsyn

The following is a preliminary listing of some of the
portraits noted during research for this book. More
investigation remains to be done.

I.  ENGRAVINGS

i)   c.1689 by Ukrainian artist Leonty Tarasevich,
with panegyric verses. Reproduced at the front of
this book. For copies and references, see: D.A.
Rovinsky, Materialy dlia russkoi ikonografii (St.
Petersburg, 1884), vyp.I, no.4 and Podrobnyi
slovar' russkikh graverov XVI-XIX vv. Vol.2 (St.
Petersburg, 1895), p.986. Rozysknye dela o Fedore
Shaklovitom i ego soobshchnikakh, vol.3 (St.
Petersburg, 1888), frontispiece. M. Semevsky,
"Sovremennye portrety Sofii Alekseevny i V.V.
Golitsyna," Russkoe slovo, 1859, no.12:411-58.

ii)  Another Tarasevich engraving, c.1689. Silvester Medvedev reported that "two Ukrainians" (Tarasevich and Ivan Bogdansky) brought Fedor Shaklovity two metal plates, with engravings of "the
Father, Son and Holy Spirit, and beneath them
figures (persony) of the sovereigns Ivan and Peter
Alekseevich and their sister the great sovereign
lady Sophia Alekseevna, and beneath them many
figures, unidentified, and on the other board a
man on a horse and another with a shield and other
figures." The horseman was identified as Golitsyn
(see references in Rozysknye dela, I, pp.546-7,
596-6, 655-62.) Recent evidence suggests that this
engraving is non-extant, although Rovinsky identified it as I. Shchirsky's Tezis Obidovskogo, Kiev,
1691 (Podrobnyi slova'. p.1232) For further discussion, see M.A. Alekseeva, "Zhanr konkliuzii v
russkom iskusstve kontsa XVII-nachala XVIIIv.," in
Russkoe iskusstvo barokko. Materialy i issledovaniia. Ed. T.V. Alekseeva (Moscow, 1977), pp.14-15.

iii)  I.Shchirsky, frontispiece to L. Baranovich,
Blagodat' i istina, 1683. Golitsyn may be depicted
as one of the mounted warriors in the left and
right foreground. A dubious attribution. See
Rovinsky, Materialy, I, no.3.

iv)  The prince on a bucking horse, in a short
tunic and plumed headdress. In G.A. Schleissing,
Derer Beyden Czaaren in Reussland, n.p. 1694,

v)   Half-portrait, holding a book with the inscription "Dogovor o vechnom mire." A copy from painting (i), below.  See Sobranie portretov rossiian, znametnitykh po svoim deianiiam. Ed. and publ. P. Beketov (Moscow, 1821), vol.I. p.164.

II.   PAINTINGS

i) Half portrait, as in (v) above, by an "unknown 17th-century artist." In the collection of the State Historical Museum (GIM), Moscow. See Ocherki istorii SSSR. Period feodalizma. XVII vek. Ed. A.A. Novosel'sky (Moscow, 1955), p.535.

ii)   Half-portrait, from the collection of the Hermitage Museum. Leningrad. Reproduced in R.K. Massie, Peter the Great. His Life and World (London, 1981), between pp.210-11.

iii)   Half-portrait, allegedly painted in Pinega, c.1710, showing the prince in wig and armour. Reproduced in N.N. Golitsyn, Rod kniazei Golitsynykh (St. Petersburg, 1892), p.120.

## INTRODUCTION

1. We use here the standard Russian version of the name, transliterated from the Cyrillic. Descendants of the clan in emigration use the spelling Galitzine. In non-Russian sources of the 17th-18th centuries attempts to render the Cyrillic in Latin script include: Galischen, Galischin, Golytsen, Golizin, Gallichen, Galliczin, Galyzin, etc. Where foreign sources have been translated into English, such variations have been replaced by the standard spelling as above.
2. See Appendix I.
3. J.H. Billington, The Icon and the Axe (London, 1966), p. 136.
4. A.Olearius, The Voyages and Travels of the Ambassadors from the Duke of Holstein, to the Grand Duke of Muscovy and the King of Persia (London, 1662), p.77, 79.
5. See, for example, D.S. Likhachev, Razvitie russkoi literatury X-XVII vekov (Leningrad, 1973), p.214.
6. F. De la Neuville, Relation curieuse et nouvelle de Moscovie (The Hague, 1699), p.55. For a discussion of this work, see below, Chapter 5, note 2.
7. S.M. Solov'ev, Istoriia Rossii s drevneishikh vremen, vol. XIV (Moscow, 1962), p.197.
8. V.O. Kliuchevsky, Kursrusskoi istorii, vol. III (Moscow, 1908), p.457.
9. V.I. Buganov, "'Kantsler' predpetrovskoi pory," Voprosy istorii, 1971, no. 10:156.
10. Billington, p.163.
11. See, for example, D. Bantysh-Kamensky, Slovar' dostopamiatnykh liudei russkoi zemli, part 2 (Moscow, 1836), pp.58-74; A.F. Malinovsky, "Biograficheskie svedeniia o blizhnem boiarine, dvorovom voevode i namestnike novgorodskom Kniaze Vasilii Vasilevich Golitsyne...," Trudy i letopisi obshchestva istorii i drevnostei rossiiskikh, 7:68-85; A. Tereshchenko, Opyt obozreniia zhizni sanovnikov upravliavshikh inostrannymi delami v Rossii, part 1 (St. Petersburg, 1837), pp.129ff; E.Serchevsky, Zapiski o rode kniazei Golitsynykh (St. Petersburg, 1853). The most thorough is A. Brückner, "Fürst W.V. Golizyn (1643-1714)", in his Beiträger zur Kulturgeschichte Russlands im XVII. Jahrhundert (Leipzig, 1887), pp.281-354.
12. De la Neuville, p.177.

CHAPTER 1

1. See the following genealogical studies: G.F. Müller, Mémoires sur l'origine et le généalogie de la maison des Princes de Galitzin (Frankfurt–Leipzig, 1762); N.N. Golitsyn, Materialy dla polnoi rodoslovnoi rospisi kniazei Golitsynykh (Kiev, 1880) and Rod kniazei Golitsynykh, vol.I (St. Petersburg, 1892).
2. Obshchii gerbovnik Vserossiiskoi Imperii (St. Petersburg, 1798). Quoted in Golitsyn, Rod, p.59.
3. Ibid., p.82.
4. Ibid., pp.115–16.
5. N. Ustrialov, Istoriia tsarstvovaniia Petra Velikogo, vol.I (St. Petersburg, 1858), p.289. See also N.N. Golitsyn, Ukazatel' imen lichnykh upomianutykh v dvorstovykh razriadakh (St. Petersburg, 1912), and Rod, p.31.
6. E.S., "Istoricheskaia mogila," Istoricheskii vestnik, 1886, no.9: 644.
7. Golitsyn, Materialy, p.56 and Rod, p.121.
8. Bol'shaia sovetskaia entsiklopediia, vol. VII (Moscow, 1972), p.16. Sovetskaia istoricheskaia entsiklopediia, vol.IV (Moscow, 1963), p.486.
9. Bantysh-Kamensky, Slovar', p.58. Serchevsky, Zapiski, p.vii.
10. N. Sakharov, ed., Zapiski russkikh liudei (St. Petersburg, 1841), p.85.
11. Golitsyn, Rod, p.119, 246.
12. Ibid., p.120. See, however, Akty istoricheskie, sobrannye i izdannye arkheograficheskoiu kommissieiu (henceforth AI), vol.V, (St. Petersburg, 1842), p.239, which records that in April 1686 Prince Vasily's cousin, Prince Ivan Ivanovich Golitsyn, held the post.
13. See below, Chapter 6, p.89.
14. Golitsyn, Rod, p.121. Drevniaia rossiiskaia vivliofika (henceforth DRV), vol.XVII (Moscow, 1791), p.205. Palace records first mention Golitsyn in 1659/60: see Golitsyn, Ukazatel', p.59.
15. DRV, XVII, p.206.
16. Golitsyn, Rod, p.121.
17. Tereshchenko, Opyt, p.134.
18. Golitsyn, Rod, p.121.
19. Ibid.
20. Tereshchenko, Opyt, p.174.
21. Golitsyn, Rod, p.129, gives the date 1680, but the birth, on August 2, 1677, is recorded in letters sent to Golitsyn by friends and relatives. See below p.12.
22. Golitsyn, Rod, p.32, 42.

23. "Chelobitnaia boiarina Kniazia Vasil'ia Vasil'evi-
    cha Golitsyna o ego sluzhbakh i po onoi vypiska i
    ukaz 1684 goda," <u>DRV</u>, XVII, pp.284 ff.
24. Ibid., pp.289-90.
25. Golitsyn, <u>Rod</u>, p.121.
26. <u>DRV</u>, XVII, p.205, 291.
27. Buganov, "Kantsler," 145. <u>Dvortsovye razriady</u>,
    vol.III (St. Petersburg, 1855), p.1641.
28. <u>DRV</u>, XVII, pp.292-93.
29. See Solov'ev, <u>Istoriia</u>, vol.XIII, p.197 ff.
30. <u>DRV</u>, XVII, p.292. Buganov, "Kantsler," 146.
31. Solov'ev, <u>Istoriia</u>, vol.XIII, p.202.
32. Ibid., pp.203-04.
33. Golitsyn, <u>Rod</u>, p.41. <u>DRV</u>, XVII, p.286.
34. <u>Polnoe sobranie zakonov Rossiisskoi Imperii</u>
    (henceforth <u>PSZ</u>), vol.II (St. Petersburg, 1830),
    no.1075, p.617.
35. Tereshchenko, <u>Opyt</u>, p.135.
36. <u>DRV</u>, XVII, p.342.
37. <u>PSZ</u>, II, no.706, pp.145-46.
38. <u>DRV</u>, XVII, p.286, 296.
39. S.K. Bogoiavlensky, <u>Prikaznye sud'i XVII veka</u>
    (Moscow, 1946), p.137, 245. Serchevsky, <u>Zapiski</u>,
    p.39. This appointment lasted for just one year.
40. <u>Tagebuch des General Patrick Gordon während seiner
    Kriegsdienst unter den Schweden und Polen vom
    Jahre 1655 bis 1661, und seines Aufenthaltes in
    Russland vom Jahre 1661 bis 1699</u>, ed. and transl
    M.A. Obolenski and M.C. Posselt, 3 vols (Moscow-
    Leipzig, 1849), I, p.413. Patrick Gordon (1635-99)
    was born in Auchleuchries, Aberdeenshire, the son
    of an impoverished laird. In 1651 he went abroad
    to seek his fortune, studying briefly at the
    Jesuit College in Braunsberg and finding employ-
    ment as a mercenary in Sweden, Poland and Aus-
    tria. In 1661 he entered the service of Tsar Alek-
    sei -- an appointment which turned out to be for
    life as the Muscovite authorities refused to re-
    lease him. He later became one of Peter I's most
    trusted friends and advisers. Gordon kept a diary,
    of which the volumes covering the years 1635-67,
    1677-78 and 1684-99 survive. Unfortunately the
    originals have never been published in full, the
    most complete version being Posselt's German
    translation, above. This version has been freely
    utilised for the present study, but it is, of
    course, rarely possible to arrive at Gordon's
    original words when translating back from the
    German. Extracts from the diary, transcribed by
    Dr. Posselt, appeared under the title <u>Passages
    from the Diary of General Patrick Gordon of Auch-
    leuchries A.D. 1635-A.D. 1699</u> (Aberdeen, 1859),

105

but the only year covered which is of direct interest to the present study is 1686. For many years the whereabouts of the original MS were unknown, but it has recently come to light in Tsentralnyi gosudarstvennyi voennoistoricheskii arkhiv (TsGIA), f.846, op.15, ed.khr. 1-7. I am indebted to Dr. Paul Dukes of Aberdeen University for bringing this to my attention and for supplying me with transcripts of passages from the year 1689, which are utilised below in chapters 5-6.

41. M.C. Posselt, Der General und Admiral Franz Lefort. Sein Leben und seine Zeit, vol.I (Frankfurt, 1866), p.301.
42. DRV, XVII, p.296-97. Gordon, Tagebuch, I, p.419.
43. DRV, XVII, p.298. Gordon, Tagebuch, I, p.420.
44. Ibid.
45. DRV, XVII, p.299.
46. A.A. Novosel'sky, ed., Ocherki istorii SSSR. Period feodalisma. XVII vek (Moscow, 1955), p.521. See also Solov'ev, Istoriia, XIII, pp.208-10.
47. DRV, XVII, pp.299-300.
48. Gordon, Tagebuch, I, p.432, DRV XVII, pp.300-01 differs, suggesting that Golitsyn's regiment arrived at Chigirin Dubrowa on August 25.
49. DRV, XVII, p.302.
50. Ibid., p.286.
51. PSZ, II, p.618.
52. Gordon, Tagebuch, I, p.450.
53. DRV, XVII, p.288.
54. Gordon, Tagebuch, I, p.454.
55. Ibid.
56. Vremennik IMOIDR, X, 1851:29-30.
57. Ibid., 47.
58. Ibid., 56.
59. Ibid., 39.
60. Russkaia starina, LVII, 1888:737-38.
61. Vremennik, VII, 1850:72.
62. Ibid., VIII, 1850:27.
63. Ibid., X, 1851:43.
64. Ibid., 56.
65. Ibid., VII, 1850:76.
66. Ibid., X, 1851:34-36, 40-41. Correspondents on this topic included his brother-in-law Prince Yu. Trubetskoy, father-in-law I.F. Streshnev, mother-in-law N.I. Streshneva, and his sister Irina.
67. Ibid., 40.
68. Ibid., 41.
69. Russkaia starina, LVII, 1888:736-37. Oriutka is a diminutive.
70. DRV, XVII, pp.305-06.
71. Gordon, Tagebuch, I, pp.485-545, gives a detailed account. See also Solov'ev, Istoriia, XIII, pp.212-15.

72. DRV, XVII, p.287.
73. i.e. September 1675-August 1677, September 1679–August 1681 (the Old Russian new year began on September 1). Ibid. p.347.
74. Dopolneniia k aktam istoricheskim (henceforth DAI), vol.IX (St. Petersburg, 1866), no.46, p.106. This appointment dated from December 1677: see Bogoiavlensky, Prikaznye sud'i, pp.176-77; Buganov, "Kantsler," 146; Bantysh-Kamensky, Slovar', p.59; Serchevsky, Zapiski, p.28.
75. DAI, IX, p. 113.
76. Ibid., p.114.
77. DRV, XVII, p.287.
78. Ibid., p.345.
79. PSZ, II, no.829, p.270.
80. DRV, XVII, pp.287-88.
81. Ibid., p.310.
82. Text in PSZ, II, nos.863, 864, pp.304-10.
83. DRV, XVII, p.310.
84. PSZ, II, no. 1075, p. 618.
85. DRV, XVII, p.310.
86. Buganov, "Kantsler," 147.
87. For texts of the Commission's report and the subsequent decree, see PSZ II, no.905, pp.368-79; Sobranie gosudarstvennykh gramot i dogovorov (henceforth SGGD), vol.IV (St. Petersburg, 1828), no.130, pp.396-410; DRV, XVII, pp.449-50; Pamiatniki russkogo prava, part VII (Moscow, 1963), pp.368-70.
88. Vremennik, XIII, 1852: 36.
89. PSZ, II, no.905, p.376.
90. Ibid., no.878 and 881.
91. Solov'ev, Istoriia, XIII, p.314. This official account (now in TsGADA, f.156, Istoricheskie i tseremonial'nye dela, d.147, l.1-16) covers events from January 12-April 27, 1682.

CHAPTER 2

1. K. Meier-Lemgo, Engelbert Kämpfer, der erste deutsche Forschungreisende 1651-1716. Leben, Reisen, Forschungen nach den bisher unveröffentlichen Handschriften Kämpfers im Britischen Museum (Stuttgart, 1937), p.14.
2. F. Adelung, Kritisch-literärische Übersicht der Reisenden in Russland bis 1700, vol.I (St. Petersburg-Leipzig, 1846), p.371. See also M.P. Pogodin, Semnadstat' pervykh let v zhizni imp-a Petra Velikogo 1672-1689 (Moscow, 1875), pp.101-02 for an analysis of Ivan's ailments. G.A. Schleissing, Derer beyden Czaaren in Reussland, Iwan und Peter Alexewiz (n.p., 1694) contains an engraving of

Ivan with a curious caul or veil over his eyes.

3. Information about the musketeer rebellion of 1682 and the events preceding it has been drawn chiefly from the following sources: Contemporary accounts: S. Medvedev, "Sozertsanie kartkoe let 7190, 91 i 92; v nikh zhe chto sodeiasia vo grazhdanstve," *Chteniia*, 1894, book 4: 1-197, and "Zapiski Sil'-vestra Medvedeva," (a shorter version) in N. Sakharov, ed., *Zapiski russkikh liudei* (St. Petersburg, 1841), pp.1-62; A.A. Matveev, "Zapiski Andreia Artamonovicha grafa Matveeva," in ibid., pp.1-94; Anon., *Diariusz zaboystwa tyranskiego senatorow Moskiewskich w stolicy roku 1682 y o obraniu dwoch carow Ioanna y Piotra* (St. Petersburg, 1901); H. Butenant, "Wahrhaftige Relation der traurigen undt schrecklichen Tragedy hier in der Stadt Moscau furgefallen Montag, Dienstag undt Mitwochen den 15, 16 undt 17 May jetzigen 1682ten Jahres," in J. Keep, "Mutiny in Moscow, 1682: a contemporary account", *Canadian Slavonic Papers*, XXIII (1981): 410-42. For a useful discussion of discrepancies in these accounts, see Pogodin, *Semnadtsat' pervykh let*, Issledovaniia, pp.3-68. A selection of documents is published in V.I. Buganov, ed., *Vosstanie v Moskve 1682 goda* (Moscow, 1976). Secondary sources include N. Aristov, *Moskovskie smuty v kontse XVII veka* (Moscow, 1871).

4. Solov'ev, *Istoriia*, XIII, p.264.

5. The daughters were Evdok'ia (b.1650), Marfa (b.1652), Sophia [Sof'ia] (1657), Ekaterina (1658), Mar'ia (1660), Feodos'ia (1662) and (by Natalia Naryshkina) Natal'ia (1673).

6. An examination of some aspects of female court life can be found in I. Zabelin, *Domashnii byt russkikh tsarits v XVI i XVII st.st.* (Moscow, 1869).

7. Solov'ev, *Istoriia*, XIII, p.184.

8. *Diariusz*, p.14.

9. J. Perry, *The State of Russia under the Present Czar* (London, 1716), p.143.

10. De la Neuville, pp.151-52.

11. Schleissing, p.15.

12. De la Neuville, p.152.

13. Voltaire, *The History of the Russian Empire under Peter the Great* (Edinburgh, 1769), p.82.

14. F. Weber, *The Present State of Russia* (London, 1723), p.138.

15. *The Antidote, or an Enquiry into the merits of a book, entitled A Journey into Siberia ... by a Lover of Truth* (London, 1772), p.115.

16. Tereshchenko, Opyt, p.147; Malinovsky, "Biograficheskie svedeniia," 69.
17. Ustrialov, I, p.26.
18. De la Neuville, p.156.
19. DRV, XVII, p.211; Golitsyn, Materialy, p.14.
20. Solov'ev, Istoriia. XIII, p.327 (from TsGADA, f.156, Ist. i tserem, dela. d.147, l.28).
21. See documents in Buganov, Vosstanie.
22. Ibid. pp.20-21.
23. Buganov, Vosstanie, pp.276-282 (with a discussion of dating, p.315). The original in TsGADA, f.156, Ist. i tserem. dela, d.147, l.37-50. See also versions in Solov'ev, Istoriia, XIII, pp.333-38 and DAI, X, no.4, pp.23-25, no.9, pp.30-32.
24. Matveev, "Zapiski", p.12.
25. Ibid., p.50.
26. Sakharov, Zapiski, p.54, note 19.
27. See Diariusz.
28. Z. Schakovskoy, Precursors of Peter the Great (London, 1964), p.158.
29. Bruckner, "Fürst," p.291.
30. Solov'ev, Istoriia, XIII, p.331. Original in TsGADA, f.156, Ist. i tserem. dela, d.147, l.34.
31. Butenant, in Keep, p.442.
32. B.I. Kurakin, "Gistoriia o tsare Petre Alekseeviche i blizhnikh k nemu liudiakh, 1682-1694," in Arkhiv Kn. F.A. Kurkaina, vol.I (St. Petersburg, 1890), p.48.
33. De la Neuville, pp.156-57.
34. Tsarstvennye bol'shie pechati i gosudarstvennykh velikikh posol'skikh del oberegatel'.
35. PSZ, II, no.358, p.471; Buganov, "Kantsler," 149. There is some dispute about the date. Solov'ev, p.367, refers to a document dated October 19, 1683 (TsGADA, f.141, Prikaznye dela starykh let, 1683 g., d.123). See also SGGD, IV, p.464, 665.
36. PSZ, II, no.1134, p.687.
37. Ibid., no.920, pp.398-401.
38. Ibid., p.401.
39. Buganov, Vosstanie, pp.36-39; Akty, sobrannye v bibliotekakh i arkhivakh Rossiiskoi imperii arkheograficheskoiu ekspeditsieiu (henceforth AAE), vol.IV (St. Petersburg, 1836), no.255, pp.358-66.
40. DAI, X, no.15, p.40.
41. See ibid., pp.37-40; Solov'ev, Istoriia, XIII, pp.343-48 (from TsGADA, f.156, d.147, l.52-66); PSZ, II, no.391, pp.412-39; DRV, XV, pp.283 ff; F. Tumansky, Sobranie raznikh zapisok i sochinenii, sluzhashchikh k dostavleniiu polnogo svedeniia o zhizni i deianiiakh gosudaria imperatora Petra Velikogo, vol.VII (St. Petersburg, 1787), pp.3-87.

42. DAI, X, pp.39-40.
43. Solov'ev, Istoriia, XIII, pp.287-88.
44. Buganov, "Kantsler," 149; Bogoiavlensky, Prikaznye sud'i, pp.58-59, 130-31, 152.
45. Buganov, Vosstanie, pp.60-69. Originals in TsGADA, f.141, Prikaznye dela starykh let, 1682g., d.111, and f.159, 1682g., d.949.
46. Buganov, Vosstanie, p.66.
47. An official account of events from August 20-October 3 appears in ibid., pp.79-107. Original in TsGADA, f.210, prikaznyi stol, st.609.
48. Buganov, Vosstanie, pp.110-11.
49. Ibid., pp.119-20, 124-25. Original in TsGADA, f.210, Moskovskii stol, st.639.
50. Buganov, Vosstanie, pp.130-33. Solov'ev, Istoriia, XIII, pp.293-95.
51. Buganov, Vosstanie, p.157; AAE, IV, no.261, p.572.
52. Buganov, Vosstanie, pp.168-70; AAE, IV, no.263, pp.376-78, no.266, pp.385-87.
53. Buganov, Vosstanie, pp.225-26; AAE, IV, no.270, pp.391-92.
54. Buganov, Vosstanie, pp.218-19; AAE, IV, no.268, pp.389-90; PSZ, II, no.961, pp.472-75.
55. See, for example, a rescript of July 9, 1682 addressed to King John Sobieski of Poland, in A. Theiner ed, Monuments historiques relatifs aux règnes d'Alexis Michaélowitch, Fédor III et Pierre le Grand Czars de Russie extraits des archives du Vatican et de Naples (Rome, 1859), p.235.
56. DAI, X, no.38, p.120.

## CHAPTER 3

1. AAE, IV, no.280, p.409.
2. Buganov, Vosstanie, pp.250-52; PSZ, II, no.1024, pp.534-35.
3. See, for example, the decree of February 13, 1683, on the restoration to their masters of serfs who had claimed their freedom during the troubles: PSZ, II, no.992, pp.499-500. Also ibid., pp.481-83, 491-92, 502-13, 551-52 et al.
4. See below, Chapter 6, p.86
5. PSZ, II, no.984, pp.490-91.
6. Ibid., no.1002, p.515.
7. Ibid., no.1004, p.516.
8. Ibid., no.1181, p.764.
9. Ibid., III, no.1335, p.15.
10. C.B. O'Brien, Russia under two Tsars, 1682-1689; the regency of Sophia Alekseevna (Berkeley, 1952), p.89.
11. Solov'ev, Istoriia, XIV, p.379.

12. N.N. Bantysh-Kamensky, Obzor vneshnikh snoshenii Rossii (po 1800) vol.III (Moscow, 1897), pp.154–55.
13. Solov'ev, Istoriia, XIV, pp.371–72.
14. Bantysh-Kamensky, Obzor, IV, pp.199–200.
15. Posselt, Lefort, I, p.341.
16. Meier-Lemgo, Engelbert Kämpfer, p.14.
17. Ibid., p.15.
18. PSZ, II, no.1059, p.570; Tumansky, Sobranie, II, p.29.
19. Adelung, Kritisch-literärische Übersicht, pp.370–71.
20. Gordon, Tagebuch, II, pp.4–11.
21. Ibid., p.10.
22. Ibid., p.14.
23. PSZ, II, no.1061, pp.575–76.
24. DAI, XI, no.14, pp.51–59.
25. Bantysh-Kamensky, Obzor, IV, p.200. Tumansky, Sobranie, IV, pp.133–35.
26. Ustrialkov, Istoriia, I, pp.119–20.
27. Ibid., pp.120–21. For a full report, see Russko-shvedskie ekonomicheskie otnosheniia v XVII veke. Sbornik dokumentov (Moscow-Leningrad, 1960), no.260, pp.443–45.
28. Ibid., no.261, pp.445–46; PSZ, II, no.1076, pp.618–22.
29. Ustrialov, Istoriia, I, p.122.
30. Ibid., p.123.
31. See Russko-shvedskie ... otnosheniia, no.263, pp.448–53 et fol.
32. Tereshchenko, Opyt, p.153.
33. Adelung, I, p.371. Theiner, p.274.
34. See Beschreibung des schauwürdigen moskowitischen Einzuges und Traktaments derer beiden Röm-kaiserl. Grossgesandten an den moskowitischen Czaren (n.p., 1684).
35. Solov'ev, Istoriia, XIV, pp.372–73. The original records of negotiations are in TsGADA, f.32, Snosheniia Rossii s Avstriei i Germanskoi Imperiei, 1684g., d.2 and 3.
36. Gordon, Tagebuch, II, p.13.
37. Theiner, pp.282–83. See also P.Pierling, Saxe et Moscou. Un médecin diplomat. Laurent Rinhuber de Reinufer (Paris, 1893), p.97.
38. Ibid.
39. PSZ, II, no.1085, pp.636–38; Bantysh-Kamensky, Obzor, I, p.235.
40. Pierling, p.33. Laurent Rinhuber first went to Russia in 1668 as assistant to a foreign doctor serving in Moscow, but subsequently took up employment as a teacher in the school in the city's foreign quarter. In 1672 he helped Pastor

Johann Gregory to organise the first theatrical performances staged at the Russian court. He left Moscow in 1672, returning in 1675-78. His own account of his journey in 1684, entitled "Wahrhafte Relation von der Moscowischen Reise," is published in Relation du voyage en Russie fait en 1684 par Laurent Rinhuber (Berlin, 1883), pp.201-76.

41. Ibid., p.211.
42. Ibid., p.222.
43. Ibid., p.226-29.  A copy of Johann Georg III's letter is located in Tumansky, Sobranie, IV, p.71.
44. Relation, pp.231-34.
45. Ibid., pp.243-44.
46. Ibid., p.248.
47. Pierling, p.101.
48. Relation, p.252.
49. Ibid., p.257.
50. Ibid., p.258.
51. Ibid., p.259.
52. DAI, XI, no.1.22, pp.74-77.
53. Solov'ev, Istoriia, XIV, pp.384-87.
54. DAI, XI, no.1, p.1.
55. Ibid., no.31, pp.109-113.
56. Ibid., X, no.51, pp.173-95.
57. Ibid., XI, no.1, p.1.
58. Ibid., XI, no.37, pp.122-23.
59. Ibid., no.40, pp.126-28.
60. Ibid., no.45, pp.133-35; no.47, pp.136-41.
61. PSZ, II, no.1082, p.625.
62. DAI, XI, no.59, pp.177-83.
63. Ibid., no.63, p.190.
64. Ibid., no.93, p.253.
65. Ibid., no.88, p.239.
66. Ibid., no.29, pp.97-109.
67. Ibid., no.90, p.243, 246-47.
68. Ibid., no.41, pp.128-129.
69. DRV, XVII, p.289. This claim of poverty is at odds with information supplied in Novosel'sky, Ocherki, p.149, 159, to the effect that under Tsar Fedor Golitsyn was granted 2,186 peasant households from crown estates.
70. DRV, XVII, pp.347,49. PSZ, II, no.1075, pp.617-22.
71. DRV, XVII, p.350.
72. Bantysh-Kamensky, Obzor, I, p.29.
73. PSZ, II, no.1131, pp.677-78.
74. Treaty in PSZ, III, no.1346, pp.31-31. An account of the negotiations appears in Solov'ev, Istoriia, XIV, pp.414-20.
75. DAI, XI, p.243.
76. Russko-shvedskie ... otnosheniia, no.271, pp.460-63.

77. DAI, XII, no.13, pp.115-16.
78. Ibid., no.20, pp.283-84.
79. Ibid., no.17, p.122 ff.
80. Gordon, Tagebuch, II, p.118.
81. Ibid., p.120; Passages, p.110.
82. Passages, p.142; Tagebuch, II, p.142.
83. DAI, XI, pp.149-52.
84. Ibid., pp.153-55.
85. See G.K. Babushkina, "Mezhdunarodnoe znachenie krymskikh pokhodov 1687 i 1689 g.g.," Istoricheskie zapiski, XXXIII, 1950: 158-72.
86. O'Brien, p.97; Kurakin, Arkhiv, I, p.52.
87. Bantysk-Kamensky, Obzor, III, p.156.
88. Ustrialov, I, p.154.
89. Ibid., pp.159-60.
90. Text in PSZ, II, no.1186, pp.770-86; Tumansky, X, pp.50 ff.
91. Ustrialov, I, p.167.
92. Solov'ev, XIV, pp.410-13.
93. Ibid., p.235.
94. Bantysh-Kamensky, Obzor, I, p.235.
95. PSZ, II, no.1187, p.786.
96. Buganov, "Kantsler," 154.
97. SGGD, IV, pp.519-25; Tereshchenko, p.161.
98. "Kak nagradit' kniazia Vasil'ia Vasil'evicha Golitsyna za okonchanie mirnykh peregovorov s Pol'sheiu," Vremennik, V, 1850, smes': 1-10.
99. PSZ, II, no.1197, p.803; DRV, XVII, pp.374-75.
100. Gordon, Tagebuch, II, p.118.
101. PSZ, II, no.1186, p.777.
102. Bantysh-Kamensky, I, p.30.
103. Georgius David, S.J., Status modernus magnae Russiae seu Moscoviae (1690), ed. and introd. A.V. Florovskij (The Hague, 1965), p.49.
104. See D. Tsvetaev, Istoriia sooruzheniia pervogo kostela v Moskve (Moscow, 1885).
105. AAE, IV, no.284, pp.419-22.
106. DAI, XII, no.17, pp.126-28.
107. Ibid., pp.128-31.
108. Gordon, Passages, p.158 and Tagebuch, II, pp.158-59.
109. Ibid., p.159 and p.160 resp.
110. Letter dated May 29, 1686. See ibid., pp.150-51 and pp.161-2 and 163-4 resp.
111. Ibid., p.160 and pp.161-62 resp.

## CHAPTER FOUR

1. PSZ, II, no.1205, p.182. Solov'ev, XIV, p.391.
2. PSZ, II, no.1224, pp.835-42.
3. Tumansky, II, p.319.
4. De la Neuville, pp.63-65.

5. Ustrialov, I, p.348. There is some doubt about the dating of this and other dispatches, published undated by Ustrialov in an appendix.
6. Ibid., p.349.
7. Ibid.
8. Ibid., p.350.
9. Ibid., pp.351-52.
10. PSZ, II, no.1231, p.847.
11. Gordon, Tagebuch, II, p.167.
12. Istoricheskoe izvestie o vsekh tserkvakh stolich-nogo goroda Moskvy (Moscow, 1796), p.153.
13. Gordon, Tagebuch, II, pp.168-69.
14. Ibid., p.170.
15. "Chin otpusku ikon i znamen v pokhod s boiarinom kniazem Vasiliem Vasil'evichem Golitsynym, 7195 (1687), fev. 22," in Tumansky, II, pp.311-20. For a list of officers in Golitsyn's regiment, see ibid., V, pp.21-39.
16. Ustrialov, I, p.194. Other sources (e.g. Posselt, Lefort, I, p.371) suggest that he left in the second half of April, but this is highly unlikely if he crossed the River Merl in early May.
17. Gordon, Tagebuch, II, p.171.
18. Ustrialov, I, pp.349-50. Belov, p.325.
19. Buganov, "Kantsler," 151; Novosel'sky, p.537.
20. Gordon, Tagebuch, II, p.176.
21. In a letter to his brother, October 1687: see Posselt, Lefort, I, p.374.
22. Ustrialov, I, p.199.
23. Gordon, Tagebuch, II, pp.175-76. See also Buganov "Kantsler," 152; Brückner, "Furst," p.321.
24. Gordon, Tagebuch, II, p.176.
25. De la Neuville, p.76.
26. Gordon, Tagebuch, II, p.180.
27. Solov'ev, XIV, pp.377-79.
28. Ibid., pp.394-98.
29. Ibid., p.398.
30. PSZ, II, no.1252, pp.863-64.
31. Ibid., no.1254, pp.967-80; Gordon, Tagebuch, II, pp.184-88; Solov'ev, XIV, pp.398-401.
32. Letter to Golitsyn in Ustrialov, I, p.356.
33. Ibid., pp.352-53.
34. See Schleissing, p.138; A. Brückner, "Materialy dlia istnochniknoveniia istorii Petra Velikogo," ZhMNP, 1879, no.8: 286.
35. "Moskva v 1687-1688. Pis'ma Kristofora fon-Kokhen, shvedskogo poslannika pri russkom dvore," Russkaia starina, 1878, no.9: 122 (henceforth Von Kochen).
36. PSZ, II, no.1258, pp.884-89.
37. Gordon, Tagebuch, II, pp.194-95.
38. Von Kochen, p.122; De la Neuville, pp.82-83; Ustrialov, I, p.353.

39. Golitsyn, Rod, p.4.
40. PSZ, II, no.1258, pp.883-97.
41. DRV, XVII, p.361.
42. Posselt, Lefort, I, pp.375-76.
43. Ibid., pp.543-54.
44. Theiner, p.328. See also a letter from Father Bonesana, a priest with the Polish army, ibid., p.329.
45. Von Kochen, p.122.
46. Ibid.
47. Gordon, Tagebuch, II, p.201.
48. DAI, XII, no.41, p.319.
49. Golitsyn, Materialy, p.20; Gordon, Tagebuch, II, p.204.
50. Ibid., p.205.
51. Ibid., p.206.
52. Von Kochen, pp.126-27.
53. Gordon, Tagebuch, II, 207.
54. Von Kochen, p.129; Theiner, pp.332-33.
55. Bantysh-Kamensky, Obzor, II, p.210.
56. Von Kochen, p.128.
57. DAI, XII, no.17, p.145.
58. Ibid., p.147.
59. Ibid., p.205.
60. Ibid., p.186.
61. Ibid., p.197, 211.
62. Gordon, Tagebuch, II, p.220.
63. Ibid., p.232.
64. Ibid., p.221.
65. Ibid., p.223.
66. Gordon, Passages, p.165 and Tagebuch, I, p.226.
67. PSZ, II, no.1313, pp.946-49.
68. Ibid., p.946.
69. Gordon, Tagebuch, II, p.230.
70. Ibid., p.233. See also SGGD, IV, no.1693, pp.587-91.
71. Brückner, "Furst," p.325.
72. Pogodin, pp.143-44.
73. Gordon, Tagebuch, II, p.237, 240-41.
74. Von Kochen, p.124.
75. Gordon, Tagebuch, II, p.209.
76. Von Kochen, p.128.
77. Letter of March 17, in Chteniia, 1911, book 4: 51-52.
78. Gordon, Tagebuch, II, pp.227-28.
79. PSZ, III, no.1338, pp.10-11; Tumansky, II, p.40.
80. Solov'ev, XIV, pp.449-50.
81. P. Avril, Travels into divers parts of Europe and Asia (London, 1693), book 4, p.14. [Transl. from Voyage en divers états d'Europe et d'Asie entrepris pour découvrir un nouveau chemin à la Chine (Paris, 1692).] The letter is dated October 8,

1687. There has been disagreement about the year of Avril's arrival in Moscow (Solov'ev, for example, dates it January, 1688), but the problem is more than resolved by numerous references to documented events of 1689 which appear in Avril's account (e.g. Peter's marriage, book 4, pp.78-79) and by an entry for January 23 in Gordon, Tagebuch, II, p.244. See also Bantysh-Kamensky, Obzor, IV, p.84, who dates their arrival January 16 and departure January 31, 1689.

82.   Avril, book 4, pp.24-26.
83.   Ibid., book 2, p.132.
84.   Ibid., book 4, pp.55-56.
85.   Ibid.
86.   G. David, "Brevis relatio revolutionis in regno Moscovitico," in J.S. Gagarin, Pater Gagarins Neueste Studieen (Stuttgart, 1857), p.133.
87.   Avril, book 4, p.175.
88.   Ibid., p.76.
89.   PSZ, III, no.1330, pp.7-8, no.1331, pp.8-9; no.1332, pp.9-10.
90.   Bantysh-Kamensky, Obzor, IV, p.85.
91.   Avril, book 4, pp.73-74.
92.   Bantysh-Kamensky, Obzor, I, p.33.
93.   Ibid., III, p.159; Avril, book 4, p.16.
94.   Gordon, Tagebuch, II, p.244.
95.   Ibid., p.248.
96.   "Doneseniia kn. V.V. Golitsyna i tovarishchei ego vo vremia krymskogo pokhoda v 1689 g.," in Ustrialov, I, p.357. Archival materials in TsGADA, f.123, Snosheniia Rossii s Krymom, kn.79.
97.   De la Neuville, pp.90-92.
98.   Ustrialov, I, p.369.
99.   Gordon, Tagebuch, II, p.258. Gordon's account breaks off on May 15, resuming on May 25, but some of the gap is filled in a letter to the Count of Errol, January 28, 1690, ibid., III, pp.235-38.
100.  De la Neuville, p.98.
101.  Copia-Schreiben des Kniar Gallicryn (sic!), Feldherrn der Moscowitischen Armee an den herrn Jablonowsky, Cron Gross-Feldherrn in Pohlen auss Perekop den 2. Jun. 1689 (Frankfort?, n.d.)
102.  Ustrialov, I. p.372.
103.  Ibid., p.377; Gordon, Tagebuch, II, p.261.
104.  Ustrialov, I, p.380.
105.  "Zapiski Ivana Afanas'evicha Zheliabuzhskogo," in Sakharov, Zapiski, p.10.
106   De la Neuville, pp.103-06. See also David, Status modernus, pp.64-65.
107.  Rozysknye dela o Fedore Shaklovitom i ego soobshchnikakh, vol.III (St. Petersburg, 1888), pp.938-39.

108. Schleissing, pp.128-29.
109. Posselt, Lefort, I, p.399.
110. Gordon, Tagebuch, II, p.263.
111. PSZ, III, no.1340, p.20.
112. AAE, IV, no.300, pp.447-50.
113. Dvortsovye razriady, IV, pp.459-65.
114. Ustrialov, I, p.383. This and the following letter were written in code. Originals in TsGADA, f.5, no.2.
115. Ibid., pp.383-84.
116. M.M. Bogoslovsky, Petr I. Materialy dlia biografii, vol.I (Moscow, 1940), p.79.
117. PSZ, III, no.1342, p.21.
118. Ibid., no.1343, p.23.
119. Ibid., p.25.
120. Ibid., no.1344, pp.30-31.
121. De la Neuville, p.110.
122. Gordon, Tagebuch, II, pp.265-66. De la Neuville, pp.110-11.
123. Gordon, Tagebuch, II, p.267.
124. Brückner, "Materialy," pp.280-83.
125. Gordon, Tagebuch, II, p.267. Quotations here and subsequently taken from a transcript of the original in TsGVIA (unpaginated). See Chapter 1, note 40.
126. Matveev, "Zapiski," p.52.
127. See analyses in Babushkina, and Buganov, "Kantsler", 153.

## CHAPTER 5

1. De la Neuville, p.34.
2. The first edition of De la Neuville's work, Relation curieuse et nouvelle de Moscovie was published in Paris in 1698. Translations appeared in Dutch (under the name Nieuwstad) in 1699 and 1707, and in English (An account of Muscovie, as it was in the year 1689) in 1699. Russian translations appeared in Russkii vestnik, III-IV, 1841, nos.3-4, and (a more accurate version) A.I. Braudo, "Zapiski de la Nevillia o Moskovii," Russkaia starina, 1891, no.9: 419-50 and no.10: 242-81. For the present work my own translations from the French version published in the Hague in 1699 have been used. De la Neuville has been mistakenly identified with the French scholar and bibliophile Adrien Baillet (1649-1706), who sometimes used the same pseudonym (see, for example, Adelung, pp.379--81, H.W. Nerhood, To Russia and Return (Ohio, 1968), p.64, et al.) Ustrialov, I, p.lxii, note 73, challenges this identification, as does Dictionnaire de biographie française, vol.IV (Paris,

117

1948), pp.1266-68. For further discussion of identity, see Pogodin, pp.72 ff. and Braudo, 9: 419 ff.

3. De la Neuville, p.181.
4. Ibid., pp.14-16.
5. Ibid., pp.160-61.
6. Ibid., pp.162-63.
7. Georgius David, "Brevis relatio revolutionis in regno Moscovitico," in J.S. Gagarin, Pater Gagarins Neueste Studieen (Stuttgart, 1857), pp.159-61.
8. De la Neuville, p.117.
9. Ibid.
10. Solov'ev, XIV, p.465.
11. Kurakin, Arkhiv, I, p.54.
12. Ibid., p.55.
13. De la Neuville, pp.158-59.
14. F.C. Weber, The Present State of Russia (London, 1723), p.38.
15. See Bogoslovsky, pp.48 ff for details of Peter's whereabouts in 1682-89.
16. Solov'ev, XIV, p.446.
17. See Pis'ma i bumagi Imp. Petra Velikogo, Vol. I (St. Petersburg, 1887).
18. Ibid., no.10.
19. Rozysknye dela, I, p.viii.
20. Voltaire, History, p.82.
21. Rozysknye dela, I, pp.116-118, 166-67 et al.
22. Tumansky, VI, pp.255-56.
23. Rozysknye dela, III, p.1096.
24. Gordon, Tagebuch, II, p.267.
25. Ibid., p.268.
26. Solov'ev, XIV, p.454.
27. Rozysknye dela, I, p.146, 756; III, p.1091, 1094, 1169 etc.
28. Gordon, Tagebuch, II, p.268.
29. Ibid., pp.269-70.
30. Matveev, "Zapiski", p.54.
31. Gordon, Tagebuch, II, p.271.
32. Ibid., p.272.
33. Ibid., p.274.
34. Solov'ev, XIV, p.459.
35. Gordon, Tagebuch, II, p.275.
36. Solov'ev, XIV, p.460.
37. Gordon, Tagebuch, II, p.278. Matveev, "Zapiski", pp.56-57.
38. Gordon, Tagebuch, II, pp.278-79.
39. Rozysknye dela, III, pp.1-2. See also the longer ukaze, ibid., pp.2-3 and versions in PSZ, III, no.1348, p.33; Solov'ev, pp.461-62; Ustrialov, II, pp.454-56.
40. Gordon, Tagebuch, II, p.281.

41. De la Neuville, p.144.
42. Gordon, Tagebuch, II, pp.281-82.
43. Rozysknye dela, III, pp.5-6.
44. Ibid., pp.7-10.
45. Ibid., pp.15-20.
46. Ibid., pp.19-24, 29-34.
47. Ibid., pp.63-69.
48. Ibid., p.79.
49. Ibid., pp.1207-08; Solov'ev, XIV, p.463.
50. Rozysknye dela, III, pp.106-7.
51. Ibid., p.92; Golitsyn Materialy, p.20 (he mentions the date November 1690).
52. Rozysknye dela, III, pp.115-16.
53. Ibid., p.113.
54. Ibid., p.127.
55. Ibid., p.133.
56. Ibid., pp.135-38.
57. Ibid., pp.139-42.
58. Ibid., pp.141-50.
59. Ibid., pp.1243-54.
60. Ibid., pp.1073-79, 1140-67.
61. Ibid., pp.1269-71.
62. Ibid., p.1273.
63. Ibid., p.1278.
64. Ibid., pp.1289-92.
65. Ibid., p.1292.
66. Ibid., p.1294. A summary of events from 15 July 1691 - 27 February 1694 can also be found in A. Vostokov, "Prebyvanie ssyl'nykh kniazei V.V. i A.V. Golitsynykh v Mezeni," Istoricheskii vestnik, 1886, no.8: 385-98.
67. Rozysknye dela, III, pp.1303-06.
68. Ibid., pp.1337-42.
69. Ibid., pp.1407-12.
70. Ibid., pp.1427-30.
71. Ibid., pp.1431-32.
72. Ibid., pp.1439-44.
73. Ibid., pp.1451-54.
74. Ibid., pp.1455-56. See also, S. Petrovsky, "Kniaz' Vasilii Vasil'evich Golitsyn," Russkia starina, 1877, no.12: 133-35.
75. E.S. "Istoricheskaia mogila," Istoricheskii vestnik, 1886, no.9: 644.
76. Ibid.
77. N.N. Golitsyn, "Po povodu zametki 'Istoricheskaia mogila'," Ibid., no.12: 668.
78. Rozysknye dela, III, pp.1455-58.
79. Ustrialov, II, p.354.
80. On Aleksei's career, see Bogoiavlensky, Prikaznye sud'i, p.245; Golitsyn, Ukazatel', p.58.
81. Golitsyn, Rod, pp.124-39, 141.

CHAPTER 6

1.  See M. Semevsky, "Sovremennye portrety Sofii Alek-
    seevny i V.V. Golitsyna. 1689," Russkoe slovo,
    1859, no.12: 411-58; Bogoslovsky, I, p.397; D.
    Rovinsky, Russkie gravery i ikh proizvedeniia s
    1564 goda do osnovaniia Akademii Khudozhestv
    (Moscow, 1870), p.295.
2.  An Impartial History of the Life and Actions of
    Peter Alexowitz the Present Czar of Muscovy: From
    his Birth down to the present Time (London, 1728),
    pp.2-3.
3.  A New History of the Life and Reign of the Czar
    Peter the Great, Emperor of All Russia, And Father
    of His Country, (London, 1740), p.51.
4.  Catherine II, Antidote, p.116.
5.  Kurakin, Arkhiv, I, p.50.
6.  O'Brien, p.xi.
7.  Ustrialov, I, p.99.
8.  Schleissing, p.126.
9.  De la Neuville, p.55.
10. Schleissing, p.127.
11. Bantysh-Kamensky, Slovar', p.59; Malinovsky, 82.
12. M.P. Alekseev, Slovar' inostrannykh iazykov v
    russkom azbukovnike XVII veka (Moscow, 1968),
    pp.145-46.
13. S.P. Luppov, Kniga v Rossii v XVII veke (Lenin-
    grad, 1970), pp.107-10. Based on analysis of mate-
    rials in Rozysknye dela, IV.
14. Luppov, pp.194-203; S. Belokurov, O biblioteke
    moskovskikh gosudarei v XVI stoletii (Moscow,
    1898), pp.66-80.
15. Bantysh-Kamensky, Slovar', p.73.
16. M. Semevsky, p.452, Belov, "Moskovskie smuty,"
    452.
17. Zheliabuzhsky, "Zapiski," p.10; Solov'ev, XIV,
    p.406.
18. Billington, pp.171-73. Documents in DAI, vol. XII,
    no.55, pp.341-43.
19. De la Neuville, p.176.
20. Posselt, Lefort, I, p.446.
21. PSZ, III, no.1351, pp.39-40.
22. David, Status Modernis, p.71; "Brevis relatio,"
    p.177.
23. Ibid., p.155.
24. Ibid., p.156.
25. O'Brien, p.51. See also Schakovskoy, p.236.
26. V.I. Semevsky, Krest'ianskii vopros v Rossii v
    XVIII i pervoi polovine XIX veka, vol.I (St.
    Petersburg, 1888), pp.1-3.
27. De la Neuville, p.215.

28. See discussion in Buganov, "Kantsler," 154-55; Kliuchevsky, III, p.460; M.Ya. Volkov, "O stanovlenii absoliutizma v Rossii," Istoriia SSSR, 1970, no.1: 101-102.
29. PSZ, II, no.992, pp.499-500.
30. Ibid., no.972, no.975.
31. See materials in Pamiatniki russkogo prava, vol. VII (Moscow, 1963), pp.185-201.
32. Ibid., pp.299-300.
33. See A.A. Stepanov, "Kniaz' V.V. Golitsyn, kak khoziain-votchinnik," Doklady Akademii Nauk SSSR, 1926, pp.45-48.
34. De la Neuville, pp.216-19, 221-23.
35. Ibid., p.178.
36. Tereshchenko, pp.150-51.
37. De la Neuville, pp.179-80.
38. Ibid., p.177.
39. PSZ, II, no.1314, pp.249-50. Similar decrees were issued in Fedor's reign.
40. L.A.J. Hughes, Moscow Baroque Architecture: a study of one aspect of Westernization in late seventeenth-century Russia. Unpublished Ph.D. thesis (Cambridge, 1976).
41. Belokurov, p.74.
42. Archimandrite Leonid, Istoricheskoe opisanie stavropigial'nogo Voskresenskogo Novyi Ierusalim imenuemogo monastyria (Moscow, 1876), pp.69-70.
43. I. Grabar', "Drevnie doma Golitsyna i Troekurova v Okhotnom riadu," Stroitel'stvo Moskvy, 1925, no.10: 12.
44. David, Status Modernus, p.89.
45. Grabar', p.13.
46. De la Neuville, p.177.
47. Published in Rozysknye dela, III and IV. MSS in TsGADA include "O moskovskom dvore Kn. V.V. Golitsyna," Prikaznye dela starykh let, f.141, 1690, no.314; 1691, no.227. "O remonte doma Kn. V.V. Golitsyna," f.110, 1691, no.1; 1692, no.1, 1697, no.1.
48. Rozysknye dela, III, pp.219-22.
49. Ibid., p.712, 729-30.
50. Ibid., IV, pp.3-5.
51. Ibid., p.10.
52. Ibid., p.11.
53. Ibid., p.13.
54. Ibid., p.22-20, 38-39.
55. Ibid., p.19.
56. Ibid., p.30.
57. Ibid., III, pp.303-10.
58. Ibid., IV, pp.176-79.
59. Ibid., p.153.

60. Ibid., III, p.487ff. on the confiscation and real-
location of these estates.
61. Ibid., pp.691-92, 703-6, 708.

## CONCLUSION

1. Brückner, "Fürst," p.281.
2. Kliuchevsky, III, p.462.
3. Brückner, "Fürst," p.353.
4. Istoricheskie pesni XVIII veka, ed. O.B. Alekseeva
   and L.I. Emel'ianov (Leningrad, 1971), pp.20-31. I
   am indebted to Ms. Elizabeth Zelensky for referring me to this work.
5. Ibid., p.20.
6. A. Brückner, "Materialy dlia istochnikovedeniia
   istorii Petra Velikogo (1682-1698)" ZMNP, 1879,
   no.8: 272-317.
7. "Zapiski o sluzhbe i nagrazhdenii Kniazia Vasil'ia
   Vasil'evicha Golitsyne," DRV, XVII, pp.284-362.

## APPENDIX I

1. Golitsyn, Rod, p.60.
2. See, for example, E.V. Kolosova et al., Lichnye
   arkhivnye fondy v gosudarstvennykh khranilishchakh
   SSSR, vol.1 (Moscow, 1952), pp.189-93.
3. Zapiski russkikh liudei. Ed. N. Sakharov (St.
   Petersburg, 1841), p.88.

BIBLIOGRAPHY

I.  PRIMARY SOURCES

(a)  PRINTED   COLLECTIONS,   INDIVIDUAL   DOCUMENTS
ETC.

Akty istoricheskie, sobrannye i izdannye arkheografi-
cheskoiu komissieiu. 5 vols. St. Petersburg,
1841-42. [AI].
Akty, sobrannye v bibliotekakh i arkhivakh rossiiskoi
imperii arkheograficheskoiu ekspeditsieiu imp.
Akademii Nauk. 4 vols. St. Petersburg, 1836.
[AEE].
Arkhiv kn. F.A. Kurakina. Vol. I. St. Petersburg, 1890.
Copia-Screibens des kniar Gallicryn, Feldherrn der
Moscowitschen Armee an den herrn Jablonowsky, Cron
Gross-Feld-herrn in Pohlen auss Perekop den 2.Jun.
1689. Frankfurt, n.d.
Dopolneniia k aktam istoricheskim. 12 vols. St. Peter-
sburg, 1846-72. [DAI].
Drevniaia rossiiskaia vivliofika. 20 vols. Moscow,
1788-91. [DRV].
Dvortsovye razriadi. 4 vols. St. Petersburg, 1855.
Istoricheskie pesni XVIII veka. Ed. O.B. Aleskseev and
L.I. Emel'ianov. Leningrad, 1971.
"Kak nagradit' kniazia V.V. Golitsyn za okonchanie mir-
nykh peregovorov s Pol'sheiu," Vremennik IMOIDR, V
(1850)
"Kniaz' V.V. Golitsyn. Pis'ma k kniaziu raznykh lits v
1677 g.," Russkaia starina, 1888, no.3: 735-8.
"Kniaz' V.V. Golitsyn. Pis'ma k nemu Boeva, Baklanov-
skogo i Leont'eva v 1677 g.," Russkaia starina,
1889, no.7: 129-32.
Pamiatniki russkogo prava. 8 vols. Moscow, 1952-63.
Monuments historiques relatifs aux règnes d'Alexis
Michaélowitch, Fédor II et Pierre le Grand, Czars
de Russie extraits des archives du Vatican et de
Naples. Ed. A. Theiner, Rome 1859.
Pis'ma i bumagi Imp. Petra Velikogo. 12 vols--
St. Petersburg/Petrograd/Leningrad, 1887
"Pis'ma k kniaziu V.V. Golitsynu," Vremennik IMOIDR, IV
(1849), V, VI, VII, VIII (1850), X (1851), XII,
XIII (1852).
"Pis'ma kn. V.V. Golitsyna k dumnomu d'iaku razriadnogo
prikaza V.G. Semenovu," Vremennik IMOIDR, V
(1850).
Polnoe sobranie zakonov rossiiskoi imperii s 1649. 1st
series. 45 vols. St. Petersburg, 1830. [PSZ].
Rozysknye dela o Fedore Shaklovitom i ego
soobshchnikakh. 4 vols. St. Petersburg, 1884-93.
Russko-shvedskie ekonomicheskie otnosheniia v XVII
veke. Sbornik dokumentov. Moscow-Leningrad, 1960.

Sobranie gosudarstvennykh gramot i dogovorov, khrani-
ashchikhsia v gos. kollegii inostrannykh del. 4
vols. St. Petersburg, 1813-28. [SGGD]
Sobranie raznykh zapisok i sochinenii, sluzhashchikh k
dostavleniiu polnogo svedeniia o zhizni i
deianiakh gosudaria imperatora Petra Velikogo.
Ed. F. Tumansky. 10 vols. St. Petersburg, 1787-88.
Vosstanie v Moskve 1682 g. Sbornik dokumentov. Ed.
V.I. Buganov. Moscow, 1976.
Zapiski russkikh liudei. Sobytiia vremen Petra Velikogo. Ed. N. Sakharov. St. Petersburg, 1841.

(b)   FOREIGNERS' ACCOUNTS

Adelung, F. Kritisch-literärische Übersicht der Reisen-
den in Russland bis 1700. 2 vols. St. Petersburg-
Leipzig, 1846.
Avril, P. Travels into divers parts of Europe and
Asia. London, 1693.
-------, Voyage en divers états d'Europe et d'Asie
entrepris pour découvrir un nouveau chemin à la
Chine. Paris, 1692.
David, Georgius, S.J. Status Modernus Magnae Russiae
seu Moscoviae (1690). Ed. and introd. A.V. Florov-
skij. The Hague, 1965.
-------, "Brevis relatio revolutionis in regno Moscovi-
tico," in J.S. Gagarin, Pater Gagarins Neueste
Studieen. Stuttgart, 1857.
Diariusz zaboystwa tyranskiego senatorow Moskiewskich w
stolicy roku 1682 y o obraniu dwoch carow Ioanna y
Piotra. St. Petersburg, 1901.
Keep, J. "Munity in Moscow, 1682:   a contemporary
account," Canadian Slavonic Papers, XXIII(1981):
410-42
"Moskva v 1687-1688 gg. Pis'ma Kristofora fon-Kokhen,
shvedskogo poslannika pri russkom dvore," Russkaia
starina, 1878, no.9: 121-29.
Meier-Lemgo, K. Engelbert Kämpfer, der erste deutsche
Forschungsreisende 1651-1716. Leben,     Reisen,
Forschungen nach den bisher unveröffentlichen
Handschrift Kämpfers im Britischen Museum.
Stuttgart, 1937.
De la Neuville, F. An account of Muscovy, as it was in
the year 1689. London, 1699.
-------, Relation curieuse et nouvelle de Moscovie. The
Hague, 1699.
-------, "Zapiski de-la Nevillia o Moskovii, 1689",
Transl. A.I. Braudo. Russkaia starina, 1891, no.9:
419-50, no.11: 242-81.
Olearius, A. The Voyage and Travels of the Ambassadors
from the Duke of Holstein, to the Grand Duke of
Muscovy and the King of Persia. London, 1662.

Passages from the Diary of General Patrick Gordon of Auchleuchries, A.D.1635–A.D.1699. Aberdeen, 1859.

Perry, J. The State of Russia under the Present Czar. London, 1716.

Pierling, P. Saxe et Moscou. Un médecin diplomat. Laurent Rinhuber de Reinufer. Paris, 1893.

Posselt, M.C. Der General und Admiral Franz Lefort. Sein Leben und Seine Zeit. 2 vols. Frankfurt, 1866.

Relation du voyage en Russie fait en 1684 par Laurent Rinhuber. Berlin, 1883.

Schleissing, G.A. Derer beyden Czaaren in Reussland. n.p., 1694.

Tagebuch des General Patrick Gordon, während seiner Kriegsdienste unter den Schweden und Polen vom Jahre 1655 bis 1661, und seines Aufenthaltes in Russland vom Jahre 1661 bis 1699. Ed. and transl. M.A. Obolenski & M.C. Posselt. 3 vols. Moscow-Leipzig, 1849.

## II.  SECONDARY SOURCES

### (a)  BOOKS

Alekseev, M.P. Slovar' inostrannykh iazykov v russkom azbukovnike XVII veka. Moscow, 1968.

Aristov, N. Moskovskie smuty v pravlenie tsarevny Sofii Alekseevny. Warsaw, 1871.

Bantysh-Kamensky, D.N. Slovar' dostopamiatnykh liudei russkoi zemli. 5 vols. Moscow, 1836.

———, N.N. Obzor vneshnikh snoshenii Rossii (po 1800 god). 4 vols. Moscow, 1894-1902.

Belokurov, S. O biblioteke moskovskikh gosudarei v XVI stoletii. Moscow, 1898.

Billington, J.H. The Icon and the Axe. London, 1966.

Bogoiavlensky, S.K. Prikaznye sud'i XVII veka. Moscow, 1946.

Bogoslovsky, M.M. Petr I. Materialy dlia biografii. 5 vols. Moscow, 1940-48.

Buganov, V.I. Moskovskie vosstaniia kontsa XVII veka. Moscow, 1969.,

Catherine II, The Antidote, or an Enquiry into the merits of a book, entitled A Journey into Siberia, ... by a Lover of Truth. London, 1772.

Dolgorukov, P.V. Rossiiskaia rodoslovnaia kniga. 4 vols. St. Petersburg, 1854-57.

———, Rossiiskii rodoslovnyi sbornik. 4 vols. St. Petersburg, 1840-41.

Golitsyn, N.N. Materialy dlia polnoi rodoslovnoi rospisi kniazei Golitsynykh. Kiev, 1880.

———, Rod kniazei Golitsynykh. Vol.I. St. Petersburg, 1892.

-------, (comp.) Ukazatel' imen lichnykh upomianutykh v dvortsovykh razriadakh. St. Petersburg, 1912.

The History of the Life of Peter the First, Emperor of Russia containing a description of Russia or Muscovy, Siberia, Crim Tatary, &c. London, 1739.

Hughes, L.A.J. Moscow Baroque Architecture: a study of one aspect of Westernisation in late seventeenth-century Russia. Unpubl. PhD thesis. Univ. of Cambridge, 1976.

An Impartial History of the Life and Actions of Peter Alexowitz the present Czar of Muscovy: From his Birth down to the present Time. London, 1728.

Istoricheskie izvestiia o vsekh tserkvakh stolichnogo goroda Moskvy, sobrannoe iz pokazanii dukhovenstva i nachal'stva. Moscow, 1796.

Kliuchevsky, V. Kurs russkoi istorii. 4 vols. Moscow, 1904-10.

Kolosova, E.V. et al. Lichnye arkhivnye fondy v gosu-darstvennykh khranilishchakh SSSR. 2 vols. Moscow, 1962.

Leonid, Archimandrite. Istoricheskoe opisanie stavro-pigial'nogo Voskresenskogo Novyi Ierusalim imenue-mogo monastyria. Moscow, 1876.

Luppov, S.P. Kniga v Rossii v XVII veke. Leningrad, 1970.

Müller (Miller), G.F. Mémoires sur l'origine et la généalogie de la maison des Princes de Galitzin. Frankfurt-Leipzig, 1762.

A New History of the Life and Reign of the Czar Peter the Great, Emperor of All Russia, And Father of His Country. London, 1740.

O'Brien, C. Russia under two Tsars, 1682-1689; the regency of Sophia Alekseevna. Berkley and Los Angeles, 1952.

Ocherki istorii SSSR. Period feodalizma. XVII vek. Ed. A.A. Novosel'sky. Moscow, 1955.

Ocherki russkoi kul'tury XVII veka. Ed. A.V. Artsikhovsky. 2 vols. Moscow, 1979.

Pogodin, M.P. Semnadtsat' pervykh let v zhizni imp-a Petra Velikogo, 1672-1689. Moscow, 1875.

Rovinsky, D. Materialy dlia russkoi ikonografii. 12 vols. St. Petersburg, 1884-91.

-------, Russkie gravery i ikh proizvedeniia s 1564 goda do osnovaniia Akademii khudozhestv. Moscow, 1870.

-------, Slovar' russkikh gravirovannykh portretov. St. Petersburg, 1872.

Schakovsky, Z. Precursors of Peter the Great. The reign of Tsar Alexis, Peter the Great's Father, and the young Peter's struggle against the Regent Sophia for the Mastery of Russia. London, 1964.

Schuyler, E. Peter the Great. Emperor of Russia. 2 vols. London, 1884.

126

Semevsky, V.I. Krest'ianskii vopros v Rossii v XVIII i pervoi polovine XIX veka. 2 vols. St. Petersburg, 1888.

Serchevsky, E. Zapiski o rode kniazei Golitsynykh. St. Petersburg, 1853.

Shchebalsky, P. Pravlenie tsarevny Sofii. Moscow, 1856.

Shumilov, V.N. Obzor dokumental'nykh materialov tsentral'nogo gos. arkhiva drevnikh aktov SSSR po istorii g. Moskvy s drevneishikh vremen do XIX v. Moscow, 1949.

Solov'ev, S.M. Istoriia Rossii s drevneishikh vremen. 29 vols. in 15. Moscow, 1962-66.

Tereshchenko, A. Opyt obozreniia zhizni sanovnikov, upravliavshikh inostrannymi delami v Rossii. St. Petersburg, 1837.

Torke, H.J. Die Staatsbedingte Gesellschaft im Moskauer Reich. Zar und Zemlja in der altrussischen Herrschafts-verfassung 1613-1689. Leiden, 1974.

A True, Authentick, and Impartial History of the Life and Glorious Actions of the Czar of Muscovy; From his Birth to his Death. London, 1730(?)

Tsvetaev, D. Istoriia sooruzheniia pervogo kostela v Moskve. Moscow, 1885.

Ustrialov, N.G. Istoriia tsarstvovaniia Petra Velikogo. 5 vols. St. Petersburg, 1858-63.

Voltaire, The History of the Russian Empire under Peter the Great. Edinburgh, 1769.

Weber, F.C. The Present State of Russia. 2 vols. London, 1722-23.

Wittram, R. Peter I. Czar und Kaiser. 2 vols. Göttingen, 1964.

Zabelin, I.E. Domashnii byt russkikh tsarits v XV i XVII stoletiakh. Moscow, 1869.

Zamyslovsky, E.E. Tsarstvovanie Fedora Alekseevicha. Moscow, 1871.

(b) ARTICLES

Babushkina, G.K. "Mezhdunarodnoe znachenie krymskikh pokhodov 1687 i 1689 g.g.," Istoricheskie zapiski, XXX (1950): 158-72.

Belokurov, S.K. "O posol'skom prikaze," Chteniia v imp. obshchestve istorii i drevnostei rossiiskikh, 1906, book 3.

Belov, E. "Moskovskie smuty v kontse XVII veka," Zhurnal ministerstva narodnogo prosveshcheniia, 1887, no.1: 99-146, no.2: 319-66.

Brückner (Brikner), A., "Fürst W.W. Golizyn (1643-1714)," in Beiträger zur Kulturgeschichte Russlands im XVII. Jahrhundert. Leipzig, 1887, pp.281-354.

——————, "Materialy dlia istochniknovedeniia istorii Petra Velikogo," <u>Zhurnal ministerstva narodnogo prosveshcheniia</u>, 1879, no. 8: 272-317.

Buganov, V.I. "'Kanstler' predpetrovskoi pory," <u>Voprosy istorii</u>, 1971, no. 10: 144-56.

Danilov, N.N. "V.V. Golicyn bis zum Staatsstreich vom Mai 1682," <u>Jahrbücher für Geschichte Osteuropas</u>, I(1936): 1-33.

——————, "Vasilij Vasil'evic Golicyn (1682-1714)," ibid., II(1937): 539-96.

Dukes, P. "Some Aberdonian influences on the early Russian Enlightenment," <u>Canadian-American Slavic Studies</u>. XIII (1979): 436-51.

Golitsyn, N.N. "Po povodu zametki 'Istoricheskaia mogila'," <u>Istoricheskii vestnik</u>, 1886, no. 12: 666-68.

Grabar', I. "Drevnie doma Golitsyna i Troekurova v Okhotnom riadu," <u>Stroitel'stvo Moskvy</u>, 1925, no.10: 11-25.

Hughes, L.A.J. "Moscow Baroque - a controversial style," <u>Transactions of the Association of Russian-American Scholars in the USA</u>, XV(1982): 69-93.

——————, "A seventeenth-century Westerniser: Prince Vasiliy Vasil'evich Golitsyn (1643-1714), "<u>Irish Slavonic Studies</u>, III(1982): 47-58.

——————, "Sophia, regent of Russia," <u>History today</u>, 1982, no.7: 10-15.

——————, L.A.J. "Western European graphic materials as a source for Moscow Baroque architecture," <u>Slavonic and East European Review</u>, LV (1977): 433-43.

Ivanov, P. "Mogila Golitsyna v Krasnogoskom Monastyre," <u>Arkhangel'skie gubernskie vedemosti</u>, 1869, no.79.

Kalishevich, Z.E. "Khudozhestvennaia masterskaia posol'skogo prikaza v XVII v. i rol' zoltopistsev v ee sozdanii i deiatel'nosti," in <u>Russkoe gosudarstvo v XVII v</u>. Ed. N.V. Ustiugov. Moscow, 1961.

Malinovsky, A.F. "Biograficheskiia svedeniia o blizhnem boiarine... kn. Vasilii Vasileviche Golitsyne," <u>Trudy i letopisi obshchestva istorii i drevnostei rossiiskikh</u> VII (1837): 68-85.

Petrovsky, S. "Kniaz' Vasilii Vasil'evich Golitsyn," <u>Russkaia starina</u>, 1877, no. 12: 133-5.

S., E. "Istoricheskaia mogila," <u>Istoricheskii vestnik</u>, 1886, no. 9: 643-4.

Semevsky, M. "Sovremennye portrety Sofii Alekseevny i V.V. Golitsyna. 1689," <u>Russkoe slovo</u>, 1859, no.12: 411-58.

Shmurlo, E. "Golitsyn, Vasilii Vasil'evich," in <u>Entsiklopedicheskii slovar'</u>, Vol. IX. St. Petersburg, 1893, pp.47-8.

Stepanov, A.A. "Kniaz' V.V. Golitsyn kak khoziain-
    votchinnik," Doklady Akademii Nauk SSSR, 1926,
    pp.45-48.
Volkov, M.Ya. "O stanovlenii absoliutizma v Rossii,"
    Istorii SSSR, 1970, no. 1.
Vostokov, A. "Prebyvanie ssyl'nykh kniazei V.V. i A.V.
    Golitsynykh v Mezeni," Istoricheskii vestnik,
    1886, no.8: 385-98.